October 2011

INFORMATION TECHNOLOGY

Critical Factors Underlying Successful Major Acquisitions

U.S. Government Accountability Office

YEARS 1921-2011
ACCOUNTABILITY ★ INTEGRITY ★ RELIABILITY

INFORMATION TECHNOLOGY

Critical Factors Underlying Successful Major Acquisitions

Highlights of GAO-12-7, a report to congressional committees

Why GAO Did This Study

Planned federal information technology (IT) spending has now risen to at least $81 billion for fiscal year 2012. As GAO has previously reported, although a variety of best practices exists to guide their successful acquisition, federal IT projects too frequently incur cost overruns and schedule slippages while contributing little to mission-related outcomes. Recognizing these problems, the Office of Management and Budget (OMB) has launched several initiatives to improve the oversight and management of IT investments.

GAO was asked to identify (1) federal IT investments that were or are being successfully acquired and (2) the critical factors that led to the successful acquisition of these investments. To do this, GAO interviewed agency officials from selected federal departments responsible for each investment.

In commenting on a draft of GAO's report, three departments generally agreed with the report. OMB and the other departments either provided minor technical comments, or stated that they had no comments at all.

View GAO-12-7 or key components. For more information, contact David A. Powner at (202) 512-9286 or pownerd@gao.gov.

What GAO Found

According to federal department officials, the following seven investments were successfully acquired in that they best achieved their respective cost, schedule, scope, and performance goals.

Investments Identified as Successful by Federal Departments

Department	Investment
Commerce	Decennial Response Integration System
Defense	Global Combat Support System-Joint, Increment 7
Energy	Manufacturing Operations Management (MOMentum) Project
Homeland Security	Western Hemisphere Travel Initiative
Transportation	Integrated Terminal Weather System
Treasury	Customer Account Data Engine 2 (CADE 2)
Veterans Affairs	Occupational Health Record-keeping System

Source: Agency data.

Department officials identified nine common factors that were critical to the success of three or more of the seven investments.

Common Critical Success Factors

1	Program officials were actively engaged with stakeholders.
2	Program staff had the necessary knowledge and skills.
3	Senior department and agency executives supported the programs.
4	End users and stakeholders were involved in the development of requirements.
5	End users participated in testing of system functionality prior to formal end user acceptance testing.
6	Government and contractor staff were stable and consistent.
7	Program staff prioritized requirements.
8	Program officials maintained regular communication with the prime contractor.
9	Programs received sufficient funding.

Source: GAO analysis of agency data.

Officials from all seven investments cited active engagement with program stakeholders as a critical factor to the success of those investments. Agency officials stated that stakeholders regularly attended program management office sponsored meetings; were working members of integrated project teams; and were notified of problems and concerns as soon as possible.

Implementation of these critical factors will not necessarily ensure that federal agencies will successfully acquire IT systems because many different factors contribute to successful acquisitions. Nonetheless, these critical factors support OMB's objective of improving the management of large-scale IT acquisitions across the federal government, and wide dissemination of these factors could complement OMB's efforts.

_____ **United States Government Accountability Office**

Contents

Letter		1
	Background	3
	Seven IT Investments Were Reported as Being Successfully Acquired	10
	Nine Factors Were Commonly Identified as Critical to the Success of Major IT Investments	19
	Concluding Observations	29
	Agency Comments and Our Evaluation	30
Appendix I	Objectives, Scope, and Methodology	32
Appendix II	Critical Success Factors	34
Appendix III	GAO Contact and Staff Acknowledgments	52

Tables

	Table 1: IT Investments Identified as Successful by Federal Departments	10
	Table 2: Commonly Identified Critical Success Factors across Seven Successful IT Investments	19
	Table 3: Decennial Response Integration System (DRIS)—Critical Success Factors	34
	Table 4: Global Combat Support System-Joint (GCSS-J)—Critical Success Factors	38
	Table 5: Manufacturing Operations Management Project (MOMentum)—Critical Success Factors	40
	Table 6: Western Hemisphere Travel Initiative (WHTI)—Critical Success Factors	42
	Table 7: Integrated Terminal Weather System (ITWS)—Critical Success Factors	45
	Table 8: Customer Account Data Engine 2 (CADE 2)—Critical Success Factors	47
	Table 9: Occupational Health Record-keeping System (OHRS)—Critical Success Factors	50

Abbreviations

CADE	Customer Account Data Engine
CBP	U.S. Customs and Border Protection
CIO	chief information officer
CMMI®	Capability Maturity Model® Integration
DHS	Department of Homeland Security
DISA	Defense Information Systems Agency
DRIS	Decennial Response Integration System
ESC	executive steering committee
FAA	Federal Aviation Administration
FEMA	Federal Emergency Management Agency
GCSS-J	Global Combat Support System-Joint
IRS	Internal Revenue Service
IT	information technology
ITIM	Information Technology Investment Management
ITWS	Integrated Terminal Weather System
LPR	License Plate Reader
MOMentum	Manufacturing Operations Management Project
NARA	National Archives and Records Administration
NNSA	National Nuclear Security Administration
NPOESS	National Polar-orbiting Operational Environmental Satellite System
OHRS	Occupational Health Record-keeping System
OMB	Office of Management and Budget
RFID	Radio Frequency Identification
SEI	Software Engineering Institute
WHTI	Western Hemisphere Travel Initiative
VA	Department of Veterans Affairs
VHA	Veterans Health Administration

G A O
Accountability * Integrity * Reliability

United States Government Accountability Office
Washington, DC 20548

October 21, 2011

The Honorable Susan M. Collins
Ranking Member
Committee on Homeland Security
 and Governmental Affairs
United States Senate

The Honorable Thomas R. Carper
Chairman
The Honorable Scott Brown
Ranking Member
Subcommittee on Federal Financial Management,
 Government Information, Federal Services,
 and International Security
Committee on Homeland Security
 and Governmental Affairs
United States Senate

Planned federal information technology (IT) spending has now risen to at least $81 billion for fiscal year 2012. As we have previously reported, federal IT projects too frequently incur cost overruns and schedule slippages while contributing little to mission-related outcomes.[1] Given the size of these investments and the criticality of many of these systems to the health, economy, and security of the nation, it is important that federal agencies successfully acquire these systems—that is, ensure that the systems are acquired on time and within budget and that they deliver the expected benefits and functionality.

This report responds to your request that we:

1. Identify federal IT investments that were or are being successfully acquired.

---

[1]See, for example, GAO, *Polar-Orbiting Environmental Satellites: With Costs Increasing and Data Continuity at Risk, Improvements Needed in Tri-agency Decision Making,* GAO-09-564 (Washington, D.C.: June 17, 2009); and *Secure Border Initiative: DHS Needs to Reconsider Its Proposed Investment in Key Technology Program,* GAO-10-340 (Washington, D.C.: May 5, 2010).

2. Identify the critical factors that led to the successful acquisition of these investments.

To address our first objective, we interviewed the chief information officers (CIO) and other acquisition and procurement officials from selected departments in order to identify one mission-critical, major IT investment[2] that was, preferably, operational, and that best achieved its cost, schedule, scope, and performance goals.

To address our second objective, we interviewed officials responsible for each investment and asked them what critical factors led to the investment's success. We then categorized the critical success factors and totaled the number of times each factor was mentioned by the department and agency officials. In order to identify common critical success factors, we generalized critical success factors that were mentioned by three or more investments. We also compared the critical success factors to the Office of Management and Budget's (OMB) *25 Point Implementation Plan to Reform Federal Information Technology Management*[3] in order to determine whether those critical success factors support OMB's efforts.

We conducted our work from December 2010 through October 2011 in accordance with all sections of GAO's Quality Assurance Framework that are relevant to our objectives. The framework requires that we plan and perform the engagement to obtain sufficient and appropriate evidence to meet our stated objectives and to discuss any limitations in our work. We believe that the information and data obtained, and the analysis conducted, provide a reasonable basis for any findings and conclusions in this product. Further details of our objectives, scope, and methodology are in appendix I.

---

[2]The Office of Management and Budget defines a major IT investment as a system or an acquisition requiring special management attention because it has significant importance to the mission or function of the agency, a component of the agency, or another organization; is for financial management and obligates more than $500,000 annually; has significant program or policy implications; has high executive visibility; has high development, operating, or maintenance costs; is funded through other than direct appropriations; or is defined as major by the agency's capital planning and investment control process.

[3]OMB, *25 Point Implementation Plan to Reform Federal Information Technology Management* (Washington, D.C.: Dec. 9, 2010).

Background

Investments in IT can enrich people's lives and improve organizational performance. For example, during the last two decades the Internet has matured from being a means for academics and scientists to communicate with each other to a national resource where citizens can interact with their government in many ways, such as by receiving services, supplying and obtaining information, asking questions, and providing comments on proposed rules.

While these investments have the potential to improve lives and organizations, federally funded IT projects can—and have—become risky, costly, unproductive mistakes. As we have described in numerous reports and testimonies,[4] although a variety of best practice documentation exists to guide their successful acquisition, federal IT projects too frequently incur cost overruns and schedule slippages while contributing little to mission-related outcomes.

IT Acquisition Best Practices Have Been Identified by Industry and Government and Promoted by Legislation

IT acquisition best practices have been developed by both industry and the federal government. For example, the Software Engineering Institute[5] (SEI) has developed highly regarded and widely used guidance[6] on best practices such as requirements development and management, risk management, configuration management, validation and verification, and project monitoring and control. In the federal government, GAO's own research in IT management best practices led to the development of the Information Technology Investment Management (ITIM) Framework,[7]

---

[4]See, for example, GAO-09-564; GAO, *Secure Border Initiative: DHS Needs to Address Testing and Performance Limitations That Place Key Technology Program at Risk*, GAO-10-158 (Washington, D.C.: Jan. 29, 2010); GAO-10-340; and *FEMA: Action Needed to Improve Administration of the National Flood Insurance Program*, GAO-11-297 (Washington, D.C.: June 9, 2011).

[5]The Software Engineering Institute is a federally funded research and development center operated by Carnegie Mellon University. Its mission is to advance software engineering and related disciplines to ensure the development and operation of systems with predictable and improved cost, schedule, and quality.

[6]See, for example, Carnegie Mellon Software Engineering Institute, Capability Maturity Model® Integration for Development (CMMI-DEV), Version 1.3 (November 2010); and Carnegie Mellon Software Engineering Institute, Capability Maturity Model® Integration for Acquisition (CMMI-ACQ), Version 1.3 (November 2010).

[7]GAO, *Executive Guide: Information Technology Investment Management, A Framework for Assessing and Improving Process Maturity*, GAO-04-394G (Washington, D.C.: March 2004).

which describes essential and complementary IT investment management disciplines, such as oversight of system development and acquisition management, and organizes them into a set of critical processes for successful investments.

Congress has also enacted legislation that reflects IT management best practices. For example, the Clinger-Cohen Act of 1996, which was informed by GAO best practice recommendations,[8] requires federal agencies to focus more on the results they have achieved through IT investments, while concurrently improving their IT acquisition processes. Specifically, the act requires agency heads to implement a process to maximize the value of the agency's IT investments and assess, manage, and evaluate the risks of its IT acquisitions.[9] Further, the act establishes chief information officers (CIO) to advise and assist agency heads in carrying out these responsibilities.[10] The act also requires OMB to encourage agencies to develop and use best practices in IT acquisition.[11]

Additionally, the E-Government Act of 2002 established a CIO Council, which is led by the Federal CIO, to be the principal interagency forum for improving agency practices related to the development, acquisition, and management of information resources, including sharing best practices.[12] Consistent with this mandate, the CIO Council established a Management Best Practices Committee in order to serve as a focal point for promoting IT best practices within the federal government.

---

[8]GAO, *Executive Guide: Improving Mission Performance Through Strategic Information Management and Technology: Learning from Leading Organizations*, GAO/AIMD-94-115 (Washington, D.C.: May 1994). See also, GAO, *Managing Technology: Best Practices Can Improve Performance and Produce Results*, GAO/T-AIMD-97-38 (Washington, D.C.: January 1997); and *Executive Guide: Measuring Performance and Demonstrating Results of Information Technology Investments*, GAO/AIMD-98-89 (Washington, D.C.: March 1998).

[9]40 U.S.C. § 11312.

[10]40 U.S.C. § 11315.

[11]40 U.S.C. § 11302(f).

[12]44 U.S.C. § 3603. The Federal CIO is the presidential designation for the Administrator of the OMB Office of E-Government, which was also established by the E-Government Act. 44 U.S.C. § 3602.

Prior GAO Work Has Identified IT Acquisition Management Weaknesses, Cost Increases, and Schedule Delays on Troubled Investments

We have often reported on a range of acquisition management weaknesses facing federal IT investments—including problems relating to senior leadership, requirements management, and testing. For example, for the investments described below, we have identified acquisition weaknesses, and have reported on significant cost increases and schedule delays. Additionally, each of these investments was ultimately cancelled or significantly restructured as a result of agency reviews conducted in response to acquisition weaknesses, cost increases, and schedule delays.

- In June 2009, we reported that an executive committee for the National Polar-orbiting Operational Environmental Satellite System (NPOESS)—a program jointly managed by the Department of Commerce's National Oceanic and Atmospheric Administration, the Department of Defense, and the National Aeronautics and Space Administration—lacked the membership and leadership needed to effectively and efficiently oversee and direct the program.[13] Specifically, the Defense committee member with acquisition authority did not attend committee meetings and sometimes contradicted the committee's decisions. Further, the committee did not track its action items to closure, and many of the committee's decisions did not achieve desired outcomes. To address these issues, we recommended that the Secretary of Defense direct the key committee member to attend and participate in committee meetings. Additionally, we recommended that the heads of the agencies that participate in the committee direct the committee members to track action items to closure, and identify the desired outcomes associated with each of the committee's actions.

  Further, we reported that the launch date for an NPOESS demonstration satellite had been delayed by over 5 years and the cost estimate for the program had more than doubled—from $6.5 billion to about $15 billion.[14] In February 2010, a presidential task force decided to disband NPOESS and, instead, have the agencies undertake separate acquisitions.

---

[13]GAO-09-564.

[14]GAO, *Polar-Orbiting Environmental Satellites: Agencies Must Act Quickly to Address Risks That Jeopardize the Continuity of Weather and Climate Data*, GAO-10-558 (Washington, D.C.: May 27, 2010).

- Since 2007, we have reported on a range of acquisition weaknesses facing the Department of Homeland Security's (DHS) Secure Border Initiative Network—also known as SBI*net*. For example, in January 2010, we reported that DHS had not effectively managed key aspects of the SBI*net* testing program such as defining test plans and procedures in accordance with important elements of relevant guidance.[15] In light of these weaknesses, we made recommendations to DHS related to the content, review, and approval of test planning documentation.

  In May 2010, we reported that the final acceptance of the first two SBI*net* deployments had slipped from November 2009 and March 2010 to September 2010 and November 2010, respectively, and that the cost-effectiveness of the system had not been justified.[16] We concluded that DHS had not yet demonstrated that the considerable time and money being invested to acquire and develop SBI*net* was a wise and prudent use of limited resources. The Secretary of Homeland Security ordered a departmentwide assessment of the SBI*net* program; the Secretary's decision was motivated in part by continuing delays in the development and deployment of SBI*net* capabilities and concerns that the SBI*net* system had not been adequately justified by a quantitative assessment of cost and benefits. Based on the results of the assessment, in January 2011, the DHS Secretary decided to end SBI*net* as originally conceived.

- In May 2010, we reported that after spending $127 million over 9 years on an outpatient scheduling system, the Department of Veterans Affairs (VA) has not implemented any of the planned system's capabilities and is essentially starting over.[17] After determining that the system could not be deployed, the department terminated the contract and ended the program in September 2009. We concluded that the department's efforts to successfully complete the system had been hindered by weaknesses in several key project management disciplines and a lack of effective oversight that, if not

---

[15]GAO-10-158.

[16]GAO-10-340.

[17]GAO, *Information Technology: Management Improvements Are Essential to VA's Second Effort to Replace Its Outpatient Scheduling System,* GAO-10-579 (Washington, D.C.: May 27, 2010).

addressed, could undermine the department's second effort to replace the scheduling system. We recommended that the department take action to improve key processes, including acquisition management, requirements management, system testing, implementation of earned value management, risk management, and program oversight.

- In June 2011, we reported that end users[18] were not sufficiently involved in defining requirements for the Federal Emergency Management Agency's (FEMA) National Flood Insurance Program's insurance policy and claims management system.[19] After conducting an assessment of the program prompted by problems identified in end user testing, FEMA leadership cancelled the system because it failed to meet end user expectations. This decision forced the agency to continue to rely on an outdated system that is neither effective nor efficient. In order to avoid the root causes of this program's failure, we recommended that for future related modernization attempts, DHS should ensure that key stakeholders are adequately involved in requirements development and management.

Additionally, we have previously reported on investments in need of management attention across the federal government. For example, in April 2011, we reported[20] on the visibility into federal IT investments provided by the IT Dashboard—a publicly available website that displays detailed information on federal agencies' major IT investments, including assessments of actual performance against cost and schedule targets (referred to as ratings) for approximately 800 major federal IT investments.[21] Specifically, we reported that, as of March 2011, the Dashboard provided visibility into over 300 IT investments, totaling almost $20 billion, in need of management attention. We noted that

- 272 investments with costs totaling $17.7 billion had ratings that indicated the need for attention, and

---

[18]End users are the individuals or groups who will operate the system for its intended purpose when it is deployed.

[19]GAO-11-297.

[20]GAO, *Information Technology: Continued Improvements in Investment Oversight and Management Can Yield Billions in Savings*, GAO-11-511T (Washington, D.C.: Apr. 12, 2011).

[21]Available at http://www.itdashboard.gov.

- 39 investments with costs totaling $2.0 billion had ratings that indicated significant concerns.

OMB Has Several Initiatives Under Way to Improve the Oversight and Management of IT Investments

OMB plays a key role in helping federal agencies manage their investments by working with them to better plan, justify, and determine how much they need to spend on projects and how to manage approved projects.

In June 2009, OMB established the IT Dashboard to improve the transparency into and oversight of agencies' IT investments. According to OMB officials, agency CIOs are required to update each major investment in the IT Dashboard with a rating based on the CIO's evaluation of certain aspects of the investment, such as risk management, requirements management, contractor oversight, and human capital. According to OMB, these data are intended to provide a near real-time perspective of the performance of these investments, as well as a historical perspective. Further, the public display of these data is intended to allow OMB, congressional and other oversight bodies, and the general public to hold government agencies accountable for results and progress.

In January 2010, the Federal CIO began leading TechStat sessions—reviews of selected IT investments between OMB and agency leadership—to increase accountability and transparency and improve performance. OMB has identified factors that may result in an investment being selected for a TechStat session, such as—but not limited to—evidence of (1) poor performance; (2) duplication with other systems or projects; (3) unmitigated risks; and (4) misalignment with policies and best practices.

OMB officials stated that as of June 30, 2011, 63 TechStat sessions had been held with federal agencies. According to OMB, these sessions enabled the government to improve or terminate IT investments that were experiencing performance problems. For example, in June 2010, the Federal CIO led a TechStat on the National Archives and Records Administration's (NARA) Electronic Records Archives investment that resulted in six corrective actions, including halting fiscal year 2012 development funding pending the completion of a strategic plan. Similarly, in January 2011, we reported that NARA had not been positioned to identify potential cost and schedule problems early, and had not been able to take timely actions to correct problems, delays, and cost increases on this system acquisition program.[22] Moreover, we estimated that the program would likely overrun costs by between $205 and $405 million if the agency completed the program as originally designed. We made multiple recommendations to the Archivist of the United States, including establishing a comprehensive plan for all remaining work, improving the accuracy of key performance reports, and engaging executive leadership in correcting negative performance trends.

Drawing on the visibility into federal IT investments provided by the IT Dashboard and TechStat sessions, in December 2010, OMB issued a plan to reform IT management throughout the federal government over an 18-month time frame.[23] The plan contains two high-level objectives:

- achieving operational efficiency, and

- effectively managing large-scale IT programs.[24]

To achieve these high-level objectives, the plan outlines 25 action items. According to OMB officials, they have taken several actions pursuant to this plan. For example, pursuant to Action Item Number 10—development of an IT best practices collaboration platform—in April 2011 the CIO Council launched an IT best practices collaboration website.[25] According to OMB, this portal provides federal program managers with access to a searchable database of program management best practices in order to promote interagency collaboration and real-time problem solving related to IT programs. The portal contains links to case studies by federal

---

[22]GAO, *Electronic Records Archive: National Archives Needs to Strengthen Its Capacity to Use Earned Value Techniques to Manage and Oversee Development*, GAO-11-86 (Washington, D.C.: Jan.13, 2011).

[23]OMB, *25 Point Implementation Plan*.

[24]The plan also outlines five subordinate goals. The high-level objective of achieving operational efficiency aligns with the goal of applying light technology and shared solutions (e.g., cloud computing, shared services across the government and consolidation of multiple organizations' data centers). The high-level objective of effectively managing large-scale IT programs aligns with the other four goals: strengthening program management; aligning the budget process with the technology cycle; streamlining governance and improving accountability; and increasing engagement with industry.

[25]Available at http://www.cio.gov/bestpractices/.

agencies demonstrating the use of best practices in managing large-scale IT systems. For example, a recent case study posted by the Social Security Administration outlined efforts to develop a cadre of highly skilled, trained, and qualified program managers to promote the success of its investments.

Seven IT Investments Were Reported as Being Successfully Acquired

According to federal department officials, the following seven investments best achieved their respective cost, schedule, scope, and performance goals.

Table 1: IT Investments Identified as Successful by Federal Departments

Dollars in millions

Department	Managing agency	Investment	Total estimated life-cycle costs
Commerce	Census Bureau	Decennial Response Integration System	$1,050.0
Defense	Defense Information Systems Agency	Global Combat Support System–Joint Increment 7	$249.9
Energy	National Nuclear Security Administration	Manufacturing Operations Management Project	$41.3
Homeland Security	U.S. Customs and Border Protection	Western Hemisphere Travel Initiative	$2,000.0
Transportation	Federal Aviation Administration	Integrated Terminal Weather System	$472.5
Treasury	Internal Revenue Service	Customer Account Data Engine 2	$1,300.0 (Transition States 1 and 2)
Veterans Affairs	Veterans Health Administration	Occupational Health Record-keeping System	$34.4

Source: Agency data.

The estimated total life-cycle cost of the seven investments is about $5 billion. Six of the seven investments are currently operational. The following provides descriptions of each of the seven investments.

Commerce Decennial Response Integration System

Investment Details

Department of Commerce—U.S. Census Bureau

Number of users:
Over 10,000 call center agents and paper data capture staff between May and July 2010

Acquisition start date:
October 2005 (prime contract award)

Operations start date:
February 2010

Total estimated life-cycle costs:
$1,050.0 million through fiscal year 2011

Acquisition costs:
$505.6 million as of June 2011

Operational costs:
$536.2 million as of June 2011

Fiscal year 2012 funding request:
N/A

Source: Agency data.

The U.S. Census Bureau is the primary source of basic statistics about the population and economy of the nation and is best known for the decennial census of population and housing. The most recent decennial census was conducted in 2010. Between March and August 2010, the Census Bureau provided assistance to respondents and captured their response data via paper and telephone agent to allow sufficient time for post-capture processing, review, and tabulation. The Decennial Response Integration System (DRIS) provided a system for collecting and integrating census responses from forms and telephone interviews. Specifically, DRIS integrated the following three primary functions:

- *Paper data capture*: Processed paper census questionnaires sent by mail from respondents. The system sorted the questionnaires and captured data from them, which were turned into electronic data.

- *Telephone questionnaire assistance*: Provided respondents with assistance in understanding their questionnaire, and captured responses for forms completed over the phone. This function utilized interactive voice response as the initial contact mechanism with an option to speak with call center representatives if needed.

- *Coverage follow up*: Contacted a sample of respondents by telephone to determine if changes should be made to their household roster as reported on their initial census return with the goal of ensuring that every person in the United States is counted once and in the right place.

To help carry out the 2010 Decennial Census, the government engaged a contractor to design, build, test, deploy, implement, operate, and maintain the systems, infrastructure, staffing, procedures, and facilities needed for DRIS. The DRIS contract was divided into three primary phases. Phase 1 included the development, testing, deployment, implementation, and support of the DRIS components needed for a 2008 Census Dress Rehearsal. Phase 2 included the nationwide deployment of the DRIS components and full-scale production operations of the paper data capture, telephone questionnaire assistance, and coverage follow up functions for the 2010 Census. Phase 3 is to address post-2010 Census DRIS component disposition and data archiving. Phase 3 was to be completed in September 2011. For purposes of our report, we focused only on the first two phases of DRIS because the DRIS system was being acquired during these phases.

In October 2009, we reported that DRIS fully implemented the key practices necessary for a sound implementation of earned value management—a project management approach that, if implemented appropriately, provides objective reports of project status, produces early warning signs of impending schedule delays and cost overruns, and provides unbiased estimates of anticipated costs at completion.[26] Additionally, we reported that, as of May 2009, the DRIS contractor was experiencing a cumulative cost underrun and was ahead of schedule; however, the life-cycle cost estimate for DRIS had increased from $574 million to $946 million. This cost increase was mostly due to increases in both paper and telephone workloads. For example, the paper workload increased due to an April 2008 redesign of the 2010 Census that reverted planned automated operations to paper-based processes and required DRIS to process an additional estimated 40 million paper forms.

Defense Global Combat Support System-Joint Increment 7

Investment Details

Department of Defense—Defense Information Systems Agency

Number of users:
20-30 joint warfighter logistician users; 13,000 single-sign-on users

Acquisition start date:
December 2007

Operations start date:
March 2009 (deployment of initial operational capability for Increment 7)

Total estimated life-cycle costs:
$249.9 million for Increment 7 through fiscal year 2014

Acquisition costs:
$74.7 million for Increment 7 as of June 2011

Operational costs:
$61.1 million for Increment 7 as of June 2011

Fiscal year 2012 funding request:
$40.9 million for Increment 7

Source: Agency data.

The Global Combat Support System-Joint (GCSS-J) Increment 7 is a system that supports military logistics operations that provide military personnel with the supplies and information they need to accomplish their missions. GCSS-J combines data, such as the location and quantity of a particular resource, from multiple authoritative data sources (e.g., Asset Visibility, Joint Operation Planning and Execution System, and Global Decision Support System) and analyzes the data to provide information needed by logistics decision makers. The end users of the system are the logisticians at the various Combatant Commands, which are made up of representatives from multiple branches, each having a geographical or functional responsibility.[27] According to Defense Information Systems Agency (DISA) officials, the analyses generated by the system enable the commanders of the Combatant Commands to rapidly make critical decisions, and to plan, execute, and control logistics operations. Additionally, the system provides other end users with single sign-on access to the individual data sources. The diverse end user group, combined with a wide spectrum of data, provides a unified supply chain for the Army, Navy, Air Force, and Marine forces in a given area, which is to help eliminate inefficiencies and provide a more useful view into the supply chain.

---

[26]GAO, *Information Technology: Agencies Need to Improve the Implementation and Use of Earned Value Techniques to Help Manage Major System Acquisitions*, GAO-10-2 (Washington, D.C.: Oct. 8, 2009).

[27]The Combatant Commands are U.S. Africa Command, U.S. Central Command, U.S. European Command, U.S. Pacific Command, U.S. Southern Command, U.S. Northern Command, U.S. Special Operations Command, U.S. Strategic Command, and U.S. Transportation Command.

DISA started GCSS-J in 1997 as a prototype. The system is being developed incrementally using Agile[28] software development—specifically, the Scrum methodology.[29] DISA is currently developing and deploying major releases for Increment 7. A total of five major releases were planned within Increment 7; Releases 7.0 and 7.1, which were implemented in March 2009 and December 2009 respectively, were the subject of our review.

To date, according to DISA, Increment 7 releases have improved performance and provided new capabilities and enhancements to existing capabilities. For example, the system provides real-time information about road conditions, construction, incidents, and weather to facilitate rapid deployment of military assets.

Energy Manufacturing Operations Management Project

Investment Details

Department of Energy—National Nuclear Security Administration

Number of users:
350 shop floor users

Acquisition start date:
January 2009

Operations start date:
September 2010 (deployment of phase 1)

Total estimated life-cycle costs:
$41.3 million through fiscal year 2030

Acquisition costs:
$6.6 million as of June 2011

Operational costs:
$137,000 as of June 2011

Fiscal year 2012 funding request:
$6.1 million

Source: Agency data.

The Manufacturing Operations Management (MOMentum) Project aims to replace a suite of aging mission-essential shop floor, manufacturing control systems at the Y-12 National Security Complex[30] that support the National Nuclear Security Administration's (NNSA) Stockpile Stewardship and Management Program. The shop floor at the Y-12 complex is responsible for the construction, restoration, and dismantling of nuclear weapon components. The core software currently used in the shop floor manufacturing control systems was deployed in the mid-1980s and will no longer be supported by the vendor on its current hardware platform beginning in 2012.

The MOMentum Project has two phases. Phase 1, which was the subject of our review, was implemented in September 2010, and is a deployment

---

[28]Agile software development is not a set of tools or a single methodology, but a philosophy based on selected values, such as prioritizing customer satisfaction through early and continuous delivery of valuable software; delivering working software frequently, from every couple of weeks to every couple of months; and making working software the primary measure of progress. For more information on Agile software development, see http://www.agilealliance.org.

[29]Scrum is one of several methodologies that are used to implement Agile software development. Scrum emphasizes developing software in increments and producing segments of functionality that are tested by, and demonstrated to, users.

[30]The Y-12 National Security Complex, located in Oak Ridge, Tennessee, is the National Nuclear Security Administration's site for conducting enriched uranium activities, producing uranium-related components for nuclear warheads and bombs, and processing nuclear fuel for the Navy.

of the Production Planning module of SAP[31] for manufacturing planning and scheduling. Phase 2 is to include the deployment of the Manufacturing Execution module of SAP software and support the execution of production schedules on the shop floor. Phase 2 is scheduled to be completed in September 2013. The implementation of the system is expected to save $6 million annually, reduce cycle times for manufacturing, remove dependencies on obsolete technology and unsupported software, and reduce administrative errors and product deviations, among other things.

Homeland Security Western Hemisphere Travel Initiative

Investment Details

Department of Homeland Security—U.S. Customs and Border Protection

Number of users:
10,000 U.S. Customs and Border Protection officers at vehicular ports of entry

Acquisition start date:
February 2007

Operations start date:
September 2008 (initial operating capability), June 2009 (full operating capability)

Total estimated life-cycle costs:
$2.0 billion through fiscal year 2019

Acquisition costs:
$343.2 million as of June 2011

Operational costs:
$255.4 million as of June 2011

Fiscal year 2012 funding request:
$80.2 million

Source: Agency data.

To facilitate inspections at the nation's 330 air, sea, and land ports of entry, the Western Hemisphere Travel Initiative (WHTI) requires all citizens of the United States and citizens of Canada, Mexico, and Bermuda traveling to the United States as nonimmigrant visitors to have a passport or other accepted document that establishes the bearer's identity and citizenship to enter the country from within the Western Hemisphere.[32] In order to implement WHTI at the land border while limiting its impact on the public, U.S. Customs and Border Protection (CBP) engaged a contractor to procure and deploy technology—including Radio Frequency Identification, License Plate Reader, and Vehicle Primary Client[33] technologies. These technologies help to provide CBP officers with law enforcement and border crossing history information for each traveler and vehicle. Initial operating capability was achieved in September 2008 when these technologies were deployed to two ports of entry. Full operating capability was achieved in June 2009 when the WHTI technology was deployed to 37 additional ports of entry. The 39 total ports of entry are high-volume land ports with 354 traffic lanes supporting 95 percent of land border traffic. After reaching full operating

---

[31]SAP is a company that develops commercial software under the same name. This software consists of multiple, integrated functional modules that perform a variety of business-related tasks.

[32]Sec. 7209, Pub. L. 108-458, Intelligence Reform and Terrorism Prevention Act of 2004 (Dec. 17, 2004), as amended; 8 U.S.C. § 1185 note. The WHTI program for land and sea ports of entry became effective on June 1, 2009, under a joint DHS and State Department final rule, 73 FR 18384, April 3, 2008. For purposes of our report, we focused only on DHS efforts to deploy WHTI at land ports of entry.

[33]According to CBP, the Vehicle Primary Client integrates vehicle and traveler information, conducts queries to law enforcement databases, and provides vehicle, traveler, query result, and crossing history information to the CBP officer.

capability, the program's scope was expanded to include deployment of technology and processes to outbound operations, inbound pedestrian processing, and border patrol checkpoint processing.[34] For purposes of our report, we focused on the program's efforts to achieve full operating capability at 39 land ports of entry.

In October 2009, we reported that WHTI fully met 6 of the 11 key practices for implementing earned value management and partially met the remaining 5 practices.[35] Practices not fully met included, for example, a master schedule with activities that were out of sequence or lacked dependencies. Nevertheless, we reported that according to program officials, the WHTI contract was completed on time and on budget. We recommended that the department modify its earned value management policies to be consistent with best practices, implement earned value management practices that address identified weaknesses, and manage negative earned value trends.

Additionally, in June 2010, we reported that program officials anticipated total funding shortfalls for the second phase of the program (which is outside of the scope of our review) for fiscal years 2011 through 2015.[36] Further, we reported that schedule delays for a CBP effort to upgrade local and wide area network bandwidth capacity at ports of entry could jeopardize program performance, particularly in terms of response times. Nonetheless, we noted that actual response times exceeded the expected performance levels from June 2009 to June 2010. We did not make any new recommendations at that time.

---

[34]These efforts are now referred to as the Land Border Integration program.

[35]GAO-10-2.

[36]GAO, *Department of Homeland Security: Assessments of Selected Complex Acquisitions*, GAO-10-588SP (Washington, D.C.: June 30, 2010).

Transportation Integrated Terminal Weather System

Investment Details

Department of Transportation—Federal Aviation Administration

Number of users:
2,210 air traffic controllers and flight support personnel

Acquisition start date:
April 1995

Operations start date:
April 2003 (initial operating capability), August 2010 (full operating capability)

Total estimated life-cycle costs:
$472.5 million through fiscal year 2029

Acquisition costs:
$296.1 million as of June 2011

Operational costs:
$24.0 million as of June 2011

Fiscal year 2012 funding request:
$5.21 million

Source: Agency data.

Initially operational since April 2003, the Federal Aviation Administration's (FAA) Integrated Terminal Weather System (ITWS) provides weather information to air traffic controllers and flight support personnel. ITWS receives observation and forecast data from the National Weather Service and combines them with data from FAA terminal sensors and sensors on nearby aircraft to integrate weather hazard information for air traffic controllers, air traffic managers, and airlines. This information is presented to end users in one integrated display. According to FAA, a prototype ITWS solution was deployed to four airports beginning in 1994. Based on those successful prototypes, FAA engaged a contractor in 1997 to design, develop, test, and deploy the ITWS system. The system was deployed to its first site in 2003; deployments to other sites continued through August 2010.

According to FAA officials, one main advantage of ITWS is that it can provide a 60-minute forecast that can anticipate short-term weather changes (such as tornadoes, thunderstorms, hail, and severe icing) that could result in airplane delays or diversions to other airports, which affect the capacities at the airports. The pre-ITWS system did not have the capability to do this. According to FAA, the implementation of ITWS increases terminal airspace capacity by 25 percent in certain weather conditions and serves to maintain capacity when it would otherwise be lost.

Treasury Customer Account Data Engine 2

The Internal Revenue Service's (IRS) Business Systems Modernization program, which began in 1999, is a multibillion-dollar, high-risk, highly complex effort that involves the development and delivery of a number of modernized tax administration and internal management systems, as well as core infrastructure projects. These systems are intended to replace the agency's aging business and tax processing systems, and provide improved and expanded service to taxpayers and internal business efficiencies for IRS. One of the cornerstone projects since the inception of the Business Systems Modernization program has been the Customer Account Data Engine (CADE), which was slated to modernize taxpayer account processing through replacement of the legacy Individual Master File, a 40-year old sequential, flat-file[37] master file processing system for individual taxpayers. In August 2008, IRS began defining a new

---

[37]A flat-file is a database system in which each database contains only one file, which is not linked to any other file. Flat-files are considered to be outdated technology.

strategy—referred to as CADE 2—which would build on the progress that the current CADE processing platform had created and leverage lessons learned to date.

IRS plans to deliver CADE 2 functionality incrementally through three phases: (1) Transition State 1, (2) Transition State 2, and (3) Target State.

Transition State 1 consists of the following two projects:

- *Daily processing*: This project is to enable IRS to process and post all eligible individual taxpayer returns filed and other transactions by updating and settling individual taxpayer accounts in 24 to 48 hours with current, complete, and authoritative data, and provide employees with timely access.

- *Database implementation*: This project is to establish the CADE 2 database, a relational database[38] that will house data on individual taxpayers and their accounts; develop a capability to transfer data from the Individual Master File to the database; and provide for the access of data from the database to downstream IRS financial, customer service, and compliance systems.

In April 2011, IRS completed the Transition State 1 detailed design phase, which includes activities such as documenting the physical design of the solution. For purposes of this report, we focused only on the IRS's efforts on Transition State 1 through the completion of the detailed design phase.

In March 2011, we reported that although IRS had taken some positive steps on defining benefits, estimating costs, and managing risks for CADE 2, it did not fully identify and disclose the CADE 2 costs and benefits.[39] Specifically, we reported that

- although IRS had identified benefits for the first phase of CADE 2, it had yet to set quantitative targets for 5 of the 20 identified benefits,

---

[38]A relational database is a system comprised of multiple files, which can be linked to each other.

[39]GAO, *Taxpayer Account Strategy: IRS Should Finish Defining Benefits and Improve Cost Estimates*, GAO-11-168 (Washington, D.C.: Mar. 24, 2011).

and had yet to finalize the benefits expected in Transition State 2 or define related quantitative targets;

- although IRS's process for developing preliminary life-cycle cost estimates was generally consistent with best practices, the agency did not perform all practices associated with credible cost estimates;

- the schedule for delivering the initial phase of CADE 2 was ambitious; and

- IRS's process for managing the risks associated with CADE 2 was generally consistent with best practices.

Our recommendations included (1) identifying all of the benefits associated with CADE 2, setting the related targets, and identifying how systems and business processes might be affected, and (2) improving the credibility of revised cost estimates.

Veterans Affairs Occupational Health Record-keeping System

Investment Details

Department of Veterans Affairs—Veterans Health Administration

Number of users:
2,000 VHA health care providers

Acquisition start date:
September 2007

Operations start date:
September 2009 (Increment 1)

Total estimated life-cycle costs:
$34.4 million through fiscal year 2015

Acquisition costs:
$11.1 million through June 2011

Operational costs:
$1.5 million through June 2011

Fiscal year 2012 funding request:
$12.2 million

Source: Agency data.

During the development of the National Flu Plan, which was released in 2006, the White House Homeland Security Council directed VA to develop an employee health tracking and management system. According to VA officials, the need for this system became urgent due to the threat of pandemic influenza in 2007. As a result, the Veterans Health Administration (VHA), working with VA's Office of Information and Technology, developed the Occupational Health Record-keeping System (OHRS). According to VA officials, OHRS was divided into two increments. The first increment consisted of a minimum feature set which represented the functionality that would provide the agency with the largest return on investment. The first increment became operational in September 2009. The second increment was intended to add functionality to the minimum feature set and to address any remaining requirements. For purposes of our report we focused on the first increment—VA's efforts to acquire the minimum feature set. OHRS was developed using Agile software development—specifically, the Scrum methodology.

OHRS serves as the electronic health record system specifically for VA employees. OHRS provides the end users (i.e., VHA employees who work in occupational health offices at VHA healthcare facilities) the ability to collect and monitor clinical data on its employees (e.g., specific immunizations and medical training) and generate reports. Additionally, a VA official stated that OHRS allows physicians to document a number of health issues related to the workforce, including training and infectious disease management. Among other things, the information in this system is used to allocate staff to appropriate patient care assignments. For example, the system can identify whether a provider has received a vaccine for a certain illness and is therefore able to treat a patient with that illness.

Nine Factors Were Commonly Identified as Critical to the Success of Major IT Investments

Nine factors were identified as critical to the success of three or more of the seven IT investments. The factors most commonly identified include active engagement of stakeholders, program staff with the necessary knowledge and skills, and senior department and agency executive support for the program. These nine critical success factors are consistent with leading industry practices for IT acquisitions.[40] Table 2 shows the nine factors, and examples of how agencies implemented them are discussed below.

Table 2: Commonly Identified Critical Success Factors across Seven Successful IT Investments

Critical success factors	Investments						
	DRIS	GCSS-J	MOMentum	WHTI	ITWS	CADE 2	OHRS
1 Program officials were actively engaged with stakeholders.	X	X	X	X	X	X	X
2 Program staff had the necessary knowledge and skills.	X		X	X	X	X	X
3 Senior department and agency executives supported the programs.	X	X		X	X	X	X
4 End users and stakeholders were involved in the development of requirements.	X	X	X		X		X
5 End users participated in testing of system functionality prior to formal end user acceptance testing.		X	X	X	X		X
6 Government and contractor staff were consistent and stable.	X	X		X	X		
7 Program staff prioritized requirements.		X	X		X		X
8 Program officials maintained regular communication with the prime contractor.	X		X	X			X
9 Programs received sufficient funding.	X			X		X	

Source: GAO analysis of agency data.

---

[40]See, for example, SEI, CMMI® for Acquisition and GAO-04-394G.

Program Officials Were Actively Engaged with Stakeholders

Officials from all seven selected investments cited active engagement with program stakeholders—individuals or groups (including, in some cases, end users) with an interest in the success of the acquisition—as a critical factor to the success of those investments. Agency officials stated that stakeholders, among other things, reviewed contractor proposals during the procurement process, regularly attended program management office sponsored meetings, were working members of integrated project teams,[41] and were notified of problems and concerns as soon as possible. For example:

- Census officials stated that the DRIS stakeholders were members of the integrated project team. Their responsibilities as members of the team included involvement in requirements development, participation in peer reviews of contractual deliverables, and review of contractor proposals.

- IRS officials told us that consistent and open communication with internal and external stakeholders has been critical to the success of CADE 2. For example, IRS officials told us that they regularly report progress made on CADE 2, as well as risk information on the program to oversight bodies, IRS executives, and IRS internal stakeholders.

In addition, officials from two investments noted that actively engaging with stakeholders created transparency and trust, and increased the support from the stakeholders. For example, NNSA officials noted that notifying MOMentum stakeholders of potential issues as soon as they were identified helped to foster transparency and trust; this included getting stakeholders' approval to use a cost- and schedule-tracking approach that was not the agency's policy, but which ultimately saved the program money and time. Additionally, CBP officials noted that communication with the WHTI stakeholders was greatly enhanced by the use of a consistent message that described, for example, the goals of the program, deployment plans, privacy implications of the Radio Frequency Identification infrastructure, and impact of the program on select groups crossing the border, including U.S. and Canadian children and Native

---

[41]OMB defines an integrated project team as a multi-disciplinary team led by a project manager responsible and accountable for planning, budgeting, procurement, and life-cycle management of the investment to achieve its cost, schedule, and performance goals. Team skills include budgetary, financial, capital planning, procurement, user, program, architecture, earned value management, security, and other staff as appropriate.

Americans. CBP officials stated that this standardization created a consistent, unified vision and ensured that the message stayed on course.

Consistent with this factor, relevant guidance[42] calls for programs to coordinate and collaborate with stakeholders in order to address their concerns and ensure that they fulfill their commitments. Active engagement with stakeholders increases the likelihood that the program will not encounter problems resulting from unresolved stakeholder issues.

Program Staff Had the Necessary Knowledge and Skills

Officials from six of the seven selected investments indicated that the knowledge and skills of the program staff were critical to the success of the program. This included knowledge of acquisitions and procurement processes, monitoring of contracts, large-scale organizational transformation, Agile software development concepts, and areas of program management such as earned value management and technical monitoring. For example:

- IRS officials stated that the Treasury Secretary utilized his critical position pay authority[43] to hire executives for CADE 2 who had demonstrated success in managing large-scale transformation efforts in accordance with best practices. Specifically, IRS officials stated that the CADE 2 program manager was previously responsible for the design, development, and implementation of several major global information technology solutions for a major corporation.

- CBP officials explained that a factor critical to the success of the acquisition was that almost every member of the team working on WHTI had a good understanding of acquisitions—some even held acquisition certifications—in addition to their understanding of program management. According to those officials, these skills contributed to effective program oversight of the WHTI contractors through all phases of the acquisition, not just during contract award.

---

[42]See, for example, SEI, CMMI® for Acquisition and GAO-04-394G.

[43]Critical position pay authority allows department leadership to set the rate of basic pay for a given critical position.

Additionally, officials from three of the seven investments also cited the use of subject matter experts' knowledge in their cognizant areas as a contributing factor to their programs' successes. For example, VA officials stated that the OHRS program relied extensively on the subject matter experts' occupational health experience—treating them as part of the development team and including them in decision making. Two investments in our sample even went one step further—by selecting the program manager from the end user organization as opposed to an individual with an IT background. For example, NNSA officials stated that they used a project manager from the end user organization as opposed to an individual from the department's information technology office. This individual had decades of experience managing shop floor control systems. As a result, he was well aware of how the work on the shop floor is done and focused on safely delivering the necessary functional requirements to the end user.

Leading guidance also recognizes that programs should ensure that program staffs acquire the knowledge and skills needed to perform the project.[44] Individuals who have developed the knowledge and skills needed for the programs are more likely to perform their roles effectively and efficiently.

Senior Department and Agency Executives Supported the Program

Officials from six of the seven selected investments identified support from senior department and agency executives[45] as critical to the success of their programs. According to those officials, these senior leaders supported the success of these programs in various ways, such as by procuring funding, providing necessary information at critical times, intervening when there were difficulties working with another department, defining a vision for the program, and ensuring that end users participated in the development of the system. For example:

- The WHTI program manager told us that the former DHS Deputy Secretary reached out to another department in order to finalize a memorandum of understanding that would be used to share

---

[44]See, for example, SEI, CMMI® for Acquisition.

[45]The term "senior department and agency executives" is used in this report to describe officials that are in the department's or agency's organizational structure, and which reside at a level above that of the programs in our sample.

information on passports and passcards needed for WHTI. According to the WHTI program manager, prior to the Deputy Secretary's involvement, the other department's efforts to collaborate on this issue were not meeting the schedule requirements of the WHTI program. That official told us that after receiving the necessary support from the other department, CBP was able to more rapidly query that department's data.

- IRS officials explained that endorsement for CADE 2 has come from the highest levels of the organization. In particular, those officials told us that the IRS Commissioner has made CADE 2 one of his top priorities. IRS officials told us that the Commissioner, through, for example, his keynote speech at a CADE 2 town hall meeting for IRS employees, has provided a clear and unwavering message about CADE 2. This speech and other activities have unified IRS employees, driven change, and removed barriers that can often impede programs of this magnitude.

In our experience,[46] strong leadership support can result in benefits to a program, including providing the program manager with the resources necessary to make knowledge-based, disciplined decisions that increase the likelihood of their program's success.

End Users and Stakeholders Were Involved in the Development of Requirements

Officials from five of seven selected investments identified the involvement of stakeholders—including end users—in the requirements development process as a factor that was critical to the success of their programs. For example:

- Census officials told us that the DRIS program management office collaborated extensively with the stakeholders and the contractor to develop requirements. For example, program management office personnel, contractor staff, and the stakeholders all worked together to analyze the requirements in order to ensure they were understood, unique, and verifiable.

---

[46]See, for example, GAO-04-394G and GAO, *Defense Acquisitions: Strong Leadership Is Key to Planning and Executing Stable Weapon Programs,* GAO-10-522 (Washington D.C.: May 6, 2010).

- VA officials told us that an OHRS end user identified a set of requirements for an occupational health system 3 years prior to the initiation of OHRS development efforts. Those officials told us that the developers worked closely with the OHRS end user representative to ensure that those requirements were still valid once the program was initiated, given the length of time since the requirements were initially identified.

Relevant industry guidance recognizes the importance of eliciting end user needs and involving stakeholders in requirements development.[47] When stakeholders and end users communicate their requirements throughout the project life cycle, the resulting system is more likely to perform as intended in the end user's environment.

End Users Participated in Testing of System Functionality Prior to Formal End User Acceptance Testing

Officials from five of the seven selected investments identified having the end users test and validate the system components prior to formal end user acceptance testing for deployment as critical to the success of their program. For example:

- DISA officials told us they used a virtual site to connect developers and end users in online testing of evolving software repeatedly during the development of GCSS-J. Using the tool, the developers were able to record the sessions, which was helpful in addressing defects identified during testing.

- CBP created a fully functional test lab facility for the WHTI program at a mock port of entry test facility constructed at an old private airport in Virginia. Using this facility, they were able to test the software that was being developed and the hardware that was being proposed. Additionally, a core end user group was established and brought to the facility multiple times a year during the acquisition to test the forthcoming technology.

Similar to this factor, leading guidance recommends testing selected products and product components throughout the program life cycle.[48] Testing of functionality by end users prior to acceptance demonstrates,

---

[47]See, for example, SEI, CMMI® for Acquisition.

[48]See, for example, SEI, CMMI® for Acquisition.

earlier rather than later in the program life cycle, that the functionality will fulfill its intended use. If problems are found during this testing, programs are typically positioned to make changes that are less costly and disruptive than ones made later in the life cycle would be.

Government and Contractor Staff Were Consistent and Stable

Officials from four of the seven selected investments stated that government and contractor organizations' personnel were consistent and stable. For example:

- DISA officials indicated that the longevity of the program management office and contractor staffs has been a contributing factor to GCSS-J's success. For example, the longevity of the staff contributed to them becoming subject matter experts in their areas of responsibility.

- CBP officials explained that key program management office staff remained consistent throughout the WHTI program. In addition, according to a CBP official, the staffs genuinely liked to work with one another and were able to collaborate effectively.

This factor is consistent with relevant guidance that espouses the importance of having adequate and skilled resources.[49] In particular, having consistent and stable staff can allow teams to keep pace with their workload, make decisions, and have the necessary accountability.

Program Staff Prioritized Requirements

Officials from four of the seven selected investments cited the prioritization of requirements as enabling the efficient and effective development of system functionality. For example:

- FAA officials told us that ITWS end users presented the development team with a "wish list" of requirements that would help them significantly. Those officials told us that end users and developers prioritized those requirements by balancing importance to the end users with the maturity of the technology. FAA officials stated that prototypes of these new requirements were developed and evaluated by end users in the field and were ultimately implemented in the initial operating capability for ITWS.

---

[49]See, for example, SEI, CMMI® for Acquisition and GAO-04-394G.

- DISA officials explained that during development, GCSS-J end user representatives met with the GCSS-J program office and the GCSS-J developer twice a week for between a full and a half day in order to identify and prioritize requirements. Those officials explained that this frequent interaction was necessary because of the short development iterations (4 to 5 weeks), at the end of which useable functionality was presented to the end users for review. The frequent prioritization ensured that the functionality most critical to the end user representative was developed, and could be deployed sooner than functionality of less importance.

Consistent with leading guidance, having prioritized requirements guides the programs in determining the system's scope and ensures that the functionality and quality requirements most critical to the end users are deployed before less-desired requirements.[50]

Program Officials Maintained Regular Communication with the Prime Contractor

Officials from four of the seven selected investments indicated that regular communication between the program management office and the prime contractor was critical to the success of the program. This communication was proactive in that there were regularly scheduled meetings between the program management office and the prime contractor, with an expectation of full and honest disclosure of problems. For example:

- Census officials stated that the DRIS program management office took a proactive, "no surprises" approach to communicating with the contractor. For example, on a monthly basis, the program management office formally documented the technical performance of the contractor based on the relevant elements of the work breakdown structure[51] and the award fee plan.[52] These reports were provided to the contractor, who in turn used the feedback to improve its technical performance. In addition, DRIS program managers and their

---

[50]See, for example, SEI, CMMI® for Acquisition.

[51]The work breakdown structure is a document that defines in detail the work necessary to complete a program's objectives.

[52]Award fees are an amount of money which a contractor may earn in whole or in part by meeting or exceeding subjective criteria stated in an award fee plan typically related to areas within quality, technical ingenuity, cost-effective management, program management, and other unquantifiable areas.

contractor counterparts met weekly to discuss significant issues. DRIS officials emphasized that the expectation of open communication and trust from senior leadership fostered an environment where issues could be freely discussed with the contractor.

- CBP officials stated that during the deployment of the WHTI technology to the ports of entry, the program management office held daily conference calls with the contractor to ensure proper coordination and the rapid resolution of problems. For example, during deployment to one port of entry it was determined that the electric system that provided power to the lanes was not adequate. This problem was quickly identified, responsibility for resolving it was assigned, and the issue was quickly resolved.

Additionally, Census and VA officials stated that ensuring a positive, non-adversarial relationship between the prime contractor and the program management office was critical to the success of the investment. Census officials noted that both the government and the contractor staff recognized that the only way for the program to succeed was for both parties to succeed.

Consistent with this factor, leading guidance recognizes the importance of communication between program officials and the contractor organizations.[53] Implementation of this critical success factor enables programs to ensure that requirements are understood and risks and issues are identified and addressed earlier rather than later in the process, thereby increasing the likelihood that the delivered system will meet its intended purpose and resulting in less costly and less disruptive changes and work efforts.

Programs Received Sufficient Funding

Officials from three of the seven selected investments explained that sufficient funding for the programs contributed to the success of those investments. Officials from two of the investments attributed funding to strong congressional support; in a third case, officials cited strong leadership from senior agency and program officials as being a factor. For example:

---

[53]See, for example, SEI, CMMI® for Acquisition.

- The WHTI program manager stated that the WHTI program received the requested funding from Congress for the 2 years leading up to the June 1, 2009, mandated implementation date. Additionally, that official told us that Congress provided 2-year money, that is, money that could be obligated over a period of 2 years. Officials told us that the 2-year money gave the program great flexibility to accommodate the inherent complexities and expenditures incurred in a multiyear deployment, and to adapt to inevitable modifications in deployment requirements (that is, additional sites, lanes, and functionality).

- IRS officials told us that the IRS Commissioner helped the CADE 2 program obtain funding. For example, those officials told us that the IRS Commissioner spoke with congressional representatives frequently in order to sustain interest and support for CADE 2.

Relevant guidance recognizes the importance of sufficiently funding IT investments.[54] Investments that receive funding commensurate with their requirements are better positioned to ensure the availability of needed resources, and therefore, deliver the investment within established goals.

The nine commonly identified critical success factors are consistent with OMB's 25-point plan to improve IT management and oversight. In particular, one high-level objective of the plan—effectively managing large-scale IT programs—aims to improve areas that impact the success rates of large IT programs across the federal government. As part of this high-level objective, the plan addresses the importance of ensuring that program management professionals have extensive experience and training, defining requirements by engaging with stakeholders, and providing senior executives with visibility into the health of their IT programs. These principles of effective IT management are reflected in the commonly identified critical success factors. For example, as previously mentioned, six of the seven agencies identified the knowledge and skills of program staff and five of seven agencies cited the involvement of end users and stakeholders in the development of requirements as critical to the success of their IT investments.

While our analysis of critical success factors identified by agencies resulted in nine commonly identified factors, agencies also identified

---

[54]See, for example, SEI, CMMI® for Acquisition.

additional factors as contributing to the success of their investments. For example:

- *Agile software development:* DISA officials stated that the use of Agile software development was critical to the success of the program. Among other things, Agile enhanced the participation of the end users in the development process and provided for capabilities to be deployed in shorter periods of time.

- *Streamlined and targeted governance:* IRS officials told us that in comparison to other IRS business systems modernization projects, the governance model for CADE 2 has been streamlined. For example, those officials stated that the CADE 2 governance structure includes an executive steering committee that, in contrast to other programs at IRS that utilize an executive steering committee, is dedicated solely to the CADE 2 program. IRS officials told us that this gives an added measure of accountability and responsibility for the successful outcome of the program.

- *Continuous risk management:* VA officials stated that the risk management strategy that the program used was critical to its success. According to the VA officials, risks were identified at daily team meetings and mitigation strategies were developed. Furthermore an official explained that risk management is built in the Agile software development process by, for example, involving the end user early and often to ensure that the requirements were as thoroughly vetted as possible.

Several of these factors are also consistent with best practices, such as the critical factors relating to risk management and governance. The full list of critical success factors and how agencies implemented them are presented in appendix II.

Concluding Observations

Although the critical success factors identified by the seven agencies were cited as practices that contributed to the success of their acquisitions, implementation of these factors will not necessarily ensure that federal agencies will successfully acquire IT systems because many different factors contribute to successful acquisitions. Nevertheless, the examples of how agencies implemented the critical success factors may help federal agencies address the well-documented acquisition challenges they face. Moreover, the critical success factors in this report also support OMB's objective of improving the management of large-scale IT acquisitions across the federal government, and wide dissemination of these factors and how agencies implemented them could complement these efforts.

Agency Comments and Our Evaluation

We received written, e-mail, or verbal responses on a draft of this report from all seven departments in our review as well as OMB. These responses are summarized below.

- The Acting Secretary for the Department of Commerce provided written comments. The department stated that the report provides a good overview and assessment of governmentwide critical factors and elements that led to the successful acquisition of IT investments. The department also provided technical comments, which we incorporated as appropriate.

- An acquisition analyst from the Department of Defense CIO Acquisition Directorate, writing on behalf of the department, provided an e-mail, which stated that the department had no comments on the draft report.

- The Director of the NNSA's Office of Internal Controls, responding on behalf of the Department of Energy, provided an e-mail stating that they agreed with the report and had no further comments. They also noted that the department is committed to supporting OMB's objective of improving the management of large-scale IT acquisitions, and that wide dissemination of the factors in our report could complement OMB's efforts.

- The Director of DHS's Departmental GAO/Office of Inspector General Liaison Office provided written comments. In its comments, the department noted that it remains committed to continuing its work with OMB to improve the oversight and management of IT investments to help ensure that systems are acquired on time and within budget, and that they deliver the expected benefits and functionality. The department further stated that it will use this report to enhance and improve the factors critical to the successful acquisition of the department's investments, such as creating a structured training program to assist in obtaining certification in the program management career field, and conducting reviews to provide insight into the cost, schedule, and performance of IT investments. The department also provided technical comments, which we incorporated as appropriate.

- The Deputy Director of Audit Relations within the Department of Transportation's Office of the Secretary provided an e-mail with technical comments, which we incorporated as appropriate.

- A program analyst within the Office of the Chief Information Officer for the Department of the Treasury, writing on behalf of the department, provided an e-mail, which stated that the department had no comments on the draft report.

- The Department of Veterans Affairs Chief of Staff provided written technical comments, which we incorporated as appropriate.

- A policy analyst from OMB's Office of E-Government and Information Technology, speaking on behalf of OMB, provided verbal technical comments, which we incorporated as appropriate.

As agreed with your offices, unless you publicly announce the contents of this report earlier, we plan no further distribution of it until 30 days from the date of this letter. At that time, we will send copies of this report to interested congressional committees; the Director of OMB; the secretaries and agency heads of the departments and agencies addressed in this report; and other interested parties. In addition, the report will be available at no charge on the GAO website at http://www.gao.gov.

If you or your staff members have any questions on the matters discussed in this report, please contact me at (202) 512-9286 or pownerd@gao.gov. Contact points for our Offices of Congressional Relations and Public Affairs may be found on the last page of this report. GAO staff who made key contributions to this report are listed in appendix III.

David A. Powner
Director, Information Technology
  Management Issues

Appendix I: Objectives, Scope, and Methodology

Our objectives were to (1) identify federal information technology (IT) investments that were or are being successfully acquired and (2) identify the critical factors that led to the successful acquisition of these investments.

To address our first objective, we selected 10 departments with the largest planned IT budgets as reported in the Office of Management and Budget's (OMB) fiscal year 2011 Exhibit 53. Collectively, these departments accounted for 88 percent of the federal government's requested total IT budget for fiscal year 2011. We then asked the chief information officers (CIO) and other acquisition and procurement officials from the departments to select one major, mission-critical[1] IT investment that was, preferably, operational and that best achieved its cost, schedule, scope, and performance goals. Seven departments[2]—the Departments of Defense, Commerce, Energy, Homeland Security, Transportation, the Treasury, and Veterans Affairs—identified successful IT investments.[3] Collectively, these departments accounted for 73 percent of the planned IT spending for fiscal year 2011.

To address our second objective, we interviewed officials responsible for each investment, asking them to identify and describe the critical factors that led to their success, and to provide examples where possible. We validated our understanding of the factors and examples collected during the interviews by providing written summaries to agency officials to ensure that their information was accurately portrayed. Because of the open-ended nature of our discussions with officials, we conducted a content analysis of the information we received in order to identify common critical success factors. We then totaled the number of times

---

[1]We defined a mission-critical IT investment as one that furthered the specific mission of the department and as such would be unique to that department. For example, we did not accept an offer by a department to review the successful development and implementation of its home website, as all federal departments have home websites.

[2]The three departments that were unable to identify an IT investment that met the criteria for this engagement were the Departments of Agriculture, Health and Human Services, and Justice. The Departments of Agriculture and Health and Human Services each identified systems that they stated met our criteria; however, GAO did not agree that the systems selected were mission critical. Justice stated that it had identified an investment that met our criteria; however, it was unable to locate key documentation and evidence needed for our review.

[3]We did not independently validate the successful aspects of the investments identified for our review by the departments.

each factor was mentioned by department and agency officials, choosing
to report on the critical success factors that were identified by three or
more investments. This resulted in our list of nine commonly identified
critical success factors. We then compared these nine critical success
factors to leading industry practices on IT acquisitions, such as the
Software Engineering Institute's (SEI) Capability Maturity Model®
Integration (CMMI®) for Acquisition, the Project Management Institute's *A
Guide to the Project Management Body of Knowledge*, and GAO's
*Information Technology Investment Management: A Framework for
Assessing and Improving Process Maturity*.[4] Finally, we compared the
nine commonly identified critical success factors to OMB's *25 Point
Implementation Plan to Reform Federal Information Technology
Management*[5] in order to determine whether those critical success factors
are related to the high-level objectives found in the plan.

We conducted our work from December 2010 through October 2011 in
accordance with all sections of GAO's Quality Assurance Framework that
are relevant to our objectives. The framework requires that we plan and
perform the engagement to obtain sufficient and appropriate evidence to
meet our stated objectives and to discuss any limitations in our work. We
believe that the information and data obtained, and the analysis
conducted, provide a reasonable basis for any findings and conclusions in
this product.

---

[4]SEI, *CMMI® for Acquisition*, Version 1.2 (Pittsburgh, Pa., November 2007); Project
Management Institute, *A Guide to the Project Management Body of Knowledge* (PMBOK
Guide), 4th ed. (Newtown Square, Pa. 2008); and GAO, *Information Technology
Investment Management: A Framework for Assessing and Improving Process Maturity*,
GAO-04-394G (Washington, D.C.: March 2004).

[5]OMB, *25 Point Implementation Plan to Reform Federal Information Technology
Management* (Washington, D.C.: Dec. 9, 2010).

Appendix II: Critical Success Factors

The following seven tables provide a description of critical success factors identified by officials with each of the investments in our sample.

Table 3: Decennial Response Integration System (DRIS)—Critical Success Factors

Critical success factor	Description
Work breakdown structure-driven program organization	The DRIS work breakdown structure[a] created a set of commonly understood terms, which facilitated communication across the program. As a result, clear lines of communication and responsibility were established within and across the government and contractor program offices. Further, Census officials told us that DRIS program management documentation, including the program's schedule, requirements, and risks, aligned with the program's work breakdown structure.
Open communication with contractor through regular reviews This supports the commonly identified critical success factor: *Program officials maintained regular communication with the prime contractor.*	DRIS program managers and their contractor counterparts met weekly to discuss significant issues. Census officials emphasized that the expectation of open communication and trust from senior leadership fostered an environment where issues could be freely discussed with the contractor. The DRIS program office formally documented and communicated the technical performance of the DRIS prime contractor on a monthly basis. The contractor used this feedback to improve its performance. In addition, the contractor invited Census officials to attend working cost review meetings prior to submitting its monthly contract performance reports.[b] Census officials noted that this provided program staff with valuable insight into the contractor's performance.
Involvement of stakeholders in integrated project teams This supports the commonly identified critical success factor: *Program officials were actively engaged with stakeholders.*	DRIS stakeholders—such as Census's Population Division, which uses census data to create products like current population estimates and future population projections—were members of the DRIS integrated project teams. As part of their responsibilities as members of these teams, stakeholders were heavily involved in, for example, the development of requirements, and review of the prime contractor's deliverables.
Government and prime contractor collaboration	According to Census officials, the contractor structured its program management office to reflect the major areas of the program's work breakdown structure, and then the government structured its program management office to mirror the contractor's. Those officials told us that the mirror organizational structures and corresponding staffing positions resulted in clear lines of responsibility and communications between the two organizations. Additionally, there was a clear understanding that if the prime contractor did not succeed, the Census would in turn not succeed. Further, Census officials told us that the prime contractor adopted the same work ethic and recognized the importance of the DRIS program to the census. This partnership resulted in open communication between the prime contractor and program officials.
Government participation in contractor working meetings	The DRIS program office staff participated in the DRIS prime contractor's working meetings. For example, Census officials participated in the prime contractor's internal integrated baseline reviews.[c] Most notably, during these reviews, both the program office and an independent division of the prime contractor assessed the adequacy of the contractor's proposed performance measurement baselines. Census officials stated that this gave the DRIS program office the opportunity to hear the DRIS prime contractor's internal criticism of the proposed DRIS baselines.

Critical success factor	Description
Stabilized funding stream This supports the commonly identified critical success factor: *Programs received sufficient funding.*	The program consistently received the amount of funding from Congress that it requested for DRIS. These officials attributed the level of funding to strong congressional support for the program.
Consistent and stable staff with prior knowledge This supports the commonly identified critical success factor: *Government and contractor staff were consistent and stable.*	The program office consisted of officials who dedicated all of their time to the DRIS program. Additionally, those officials told us that many of the key Census officials in the DRIS program were involved in the 2000 Census. Census officials explained that the experienced staff provided expertise in the areas of paper capture technology and operations, quality assurance, call center tools and operations, and acquisitions and contract surveillance. Moreover, those officials stated that the DRIS prime contractor had experience on the 2000 Census. Census officials stated that the contractor's prior experience contributed to a stable paper capture system for DRIS and staff that were familiar with Census operations.
Early focus on managing risk	Risks were identified and mitigation strategies were prepared early in the acquisition in order to help define criteria for evaluating the proposals put forth by the potential DRIS developers. For example, the DRIS program identified information security as a significant risk to the acquisition. Consequently, program officials required potential developers to discuss information security issues during their oral presentations before the DRIS Source Selection Board.
Contract with properly aligned incentives	The DRIS prime contract utilized an award fee[d] contract that included clear monetary incentives for the contractor to support a successful census. For example, Census officials stated that issues with the DRIS prime contractor's technical performance—one of the factors considered in the award fee structure—were quickly addressed by the prime contractor. Risk areas for the program were a factor used to determine the incentives.
Contract with clearly defined program phases	Census officials explained that because the DRIS project had three distinct phases covering a number of years, they created a contract that could evolve over time to address changes without the program being locked into one approach early on. As a result, they created a contract that could evolve to incorporate changing requirements, integrate the results of early testing, and provide a cost and schedule measurement baseline that could be updated in order to measure performance.
Cross training of business and technical staff This supports the commonly identified critical success factor: *Program staff had the necessary knowledge and skills.*	Program officials that held a technical role on the DRIS program were trained in business skills, and officials that held a business role on the program were trained in technical skills. Those officials noted that the technical training consisted of mostly on-the-job learning; the business training was a combination of classroom and on-the-job learning.
Program office and stakeholder involvement in requirements development This supports the commonly identified critical success factor: *End users and stakeholders were involved in the development of requirements.*	The DRIS program management office, stakeholders, and the contractor collaborated extensively to develop the DRIS requirements. For example, those officials told us that the program office, stakeholders, and the prime contractor analyzed the DRIS requirements to ensure that all parties had a common understanding of the requirements, that each requirement was unique, and that each requirement was verifiable.
Program staff trained in contracting and earned value management This supports the commonly identified critical success factor: *Program staff had the necessary knowledge and skills.*	Census officials stated that all DRIS program staff that performed surveillance on the prime contractor (i.e., oversight of the services being performed by the contractor) were trained as contracting officer's technical representatives.[e] Additionally, those officials told us that DRIS program office officials were also trained in earned value management,[f] source selection evaluations, and technical monitoring as appropriate. Many of the staff held program management certifications form the Census Bureau's project management training program.

Critical success factor	Description
Operational metrics drove activities	The program office and the prime contractor were unified in their efforts to satisfy the DRIS operational metrics because those metrics represented what needed to be done to ensure the success of the Census.
Incremental releases of requests for proposals	Census officials stated that they released sections of the DRIS request for proposals in draft form in order to allow for questions from prospective contractors and early feedback from DRIS stakeholders, including those involved in investment approval at the Census Bureau and the Department of Commerce. Those officials explained that the incremental releases and subsequent comments gave the program office an early opportunity to understand possible DRIS approaches. This also allowed the program to obtain the investment approvals and award the contract on schedule.
Defined forums for resolving risks and issues	Each of the DRIS program's many meetings served a purpose and was held according to a defined schedule. For example, on a weekly basis, an overarching DRIS integrated project team met to discuss issues that were elevated from lower-level integrated project teams. Additionally, the purpose of each meeting was well known, and the participants were clearly defined. As such, those officials told us that DRIS team members knew where issues should be discussed and did not need to scramble to schedule meetings when an issue arose.
Focus on data quality	Data quality was important from the very beginning of DRIS. For example, during the source selection process, the DRIS program management office provided a standard test deck of completed Census paper questionnaires to all potential developers and required them to use their prototype solution to scan this test deck in order to demonstrate the accuracy of their proposal. During the presentations, each potential developer had to discuss the data quality results from their demonstration. Additionally, an independent contractor was hired to perform independent verification and validation on the operational results of the DRIS prime contractor's paper data capture during the 2010 Census.
Establish and update systems acquisition processes	Census-wide organizational systems acquisition processes had not been developed when DRIS was being acquired. In the absence of agency guidance, the DRIS program implemented processes from the following sources: Capability Maturity Model® Integration, best practices learned from the 2000 Census; the Seven Steps to Performance Based Contracting; relevant GAO reports; and the DRIS prime contractor's processes. The flexibility to tailor the program management processes to meet the program's specific needs contributed to the successful implementation of processes such as risk management and change management. Additionally, Census officials explained that they took steps to update and modify DRIS systems acquisition processes in order to ensure their quality. Specifically, the DRIS staff performed a "gap analysis" of the processes that they did have in place and identified processes that they needed to add. In many cases they decided to use the prime contractor's processes to fill the gaps. They also implemented a process quality assurance effort that examined one process each month to ensure that they were following the process and to solicit ideas for improving the process. In addition, on an annual basis, the DRIS program office hired an independent support contractor to review its quality assurance process in order to identify potential areas of improvement to the overall program.
Effective change control process	Census officials stated that two factors led to a change process that allowed the program to effectively control change: (1) the clear understanding of the current baseline and (2) having a change control process that was integrated with the contractor's process and which did not include unnecessary steps. Those officials added that the DRIS program performed a detailed review of each proposed change regardless of whether it was within or outside of the scope of the program.

Critical success factor	Description
Stopped work to replan due to contract funding	After the identification of a misalignment between Census and the prime contractor's anticipated contract funding soon after the DRIS prime contract was awarded, the program office stopped all work on the contract and worked with the prime contractor to replan the work to be performed. Census officials emphasized that it was important to stop all work so that the necessary attention and focus could be devoted to developing the replan, instead of trying to do both tasks at once.
Support contractor staff provided crucial skill sets This supports the commonly identified critical success factor: *Program staff had the necessary knowledge and skills.*	Census officials stated that the DRIS contractor support staff provided skill sets that were not fully possessed by the government staff, including systems architecture and information security.
Senior leadership support This supports the commonly identified critical success factor: *Senior department and agency executives supported the program.*	DRIS officials stated that involvement from Census senior leadership contributed to the success of DRIS. For example, the division chief of the Decennial Systems Contract Management Office (outside of the program management office), provided valuable information during development and testing. In addition, the Census Comptroller provided support on issues pertaining to the DRIS budget. Further, the head of the Acquisition Division helped with key pre-award and contract management challenges.

Source: GAO analysis of agency data.

[a]The work breakdown structure is a document that defines the work necessary to complete a program's objectives.

[b]The contract performance report is the primary report of cost and schedule status and provides programs with information needed for effective program control. In particular, the report provides cost and schedule variances, based on actual performance against the plan, which can be further examined to understand the causes of any differences.

[c]An integrated baseline review is held to validate that the contractor's performance measurement baseline is adequate and realistically portrays all authorized work according to schedule.

[d]"Cost-plus-award-fee" contracts provide for the reimbursement of allowable costs, plus a base fee, fixed at the contract's inception (which may be zero) and an award amount that the government determines to be sufficient to motivate excellence in performance.

[e]Contracting Officer's Technical Representatives review contractor performance regularly, ensure that contractual milestones are met and standards are being maintained, conduct regular inspections of contractor deliverables throughout the contract period, and ensure that all contract conditions and clauses are acted upon.

[f]Earned value management is a project management approach that, if implemented appropriately, provides objective reports of project status, produces early warning signs of impending schedule delays and cost overruns, and provides unbiased estimates of anticipated costs at completion.

Table 4: Global Combat Support System-Joint (GCSS-J)—Critical Success Factors

Critical success factor	Description
Stakeholder support This supports the commonly identified critical success factor: *Program officials were actively engaged with stakeholders.*	Defense Information Systems Agency (DISA) officials explained that stakeholder[a] support was critical to the successful implementation of Agile software development.[b] This support was critical because Agile introduced practices that were different from the traditional approach. For example, Agile required the continuous involvement of stakeholders in requirements development. A senior official participated in the requirements development process and also provided incentives for other stakeholders to participate as well.
Functional sponsor involvement in requirements identification and prioritization This supports the following two commonly identified critical success factors: *End users and stakeholders were involved in the development of requirements* and *Program staff prioritized requirements.*	DISA officials indicated that at the beginning of each sprint[c] the Functional Requirements Working Group, consisting of representatives from the functional sponsor, the program management office, and the contractor, met to identify which requirements were to be addressed in the release. During development the group also met twice a week for a half to full day.
Agile software development practices	DISA officials stated that the use of Agile software development was critical to the success of the program. Among other things, Agile enhanced the participation of the end users in the development process and provided for capabilities to be deployed in shorter periods of time.
Mission-focused testing This supports the commonly identified critical success factor: *Users participated in testing of system functionality prior to formal user acceptance.*	DISA officials stated that testing the system based on its ability to allow end users to perform operational tasks in support of a realistic mission was critical to the program's success. An example would be listing all of the individual steps required to load a weapon. Additionally, having the end users participate in testing at the end of each sprint helped to keep end users involved in the development process.
Integration of Agile characteristics into operational testing	DISA officials stated that integrating Agile software development characteristics into their operational testing was critical to the success of the program. Specifically, after the release went operational, the operational testers continued to collect metrics on system performance by reviewing system logs, metrics, help desk reports, remedy tickets, and problem reports to identify areas for further evaluation. For example, even though the system may have gone through the testing processes successfully, if there were an abnormally large number of end user calls a day on a certain issue during operations, the operational testers would look at their testing processes to see if there was something that they missed and how they could improve testing procedures in the future. In this way, operational testing was never "over."
Review board oversight	According to the DISA officials, because of the Agile software development process, the program underwent more frequent reviews that resulted in a more valid indicator of the status of the release. More frequent reviews allowed the GCSS-J stakeholders the benefit of participating frequently in the decision-making process, permitting real-time resolution of issues and problems and thus enabling the rapid release of functionality. Additionally, the officials indicated that they were able to decrease the turnaround time for certain tasks because the Milestone Decision Authority[d] had been delegated to DISA, as opposed to being at the Office of the Secretary of Defense level.

Critical success factor	Description
Delegation of accountability and authority	DISA officials indicated that there was empowerment to perform tasks at the lowest level. For example, the program management office was able to add pages indicating the changes that had been made to the Test and Evaluation Master Plan instead of creating a new document for each release. Additionally, according to the officials, changes to the testing process resulted in the testing period being reduced from 6 to 8 months to 2 months.
Government and contractor organizations experienced limited turnover This supports the commonly identified critical success factor: *Government and contractor staff were consistent and stable.*	A DISA official noted that the longevity of the team contributed to the success of the program. The official noted that many of the civilian staff are with the program "for life," and that the support and development contractors also have been with the program for a long time. Additionally, the longevity of the team resulted in the staff becoming subject matter experts in supporting and managing the program. For example, the Systems Design and Development Branch Chief has been with the program since 1998, and her initial duties focused on analyzing and understanding how the data the system obtained could be used. As a result, she is now a subject matter expert for issues related to the system's data.

Source: GAO analysis of agency data.

[a]A stakeholder is an individual or group with an interest in the success of an organization in delivering intended results and maintaining the viability of its products and services.

[b]Agile software development is not a set of tools or a single methodology, but a philosophy based on selected values, such as prioritizing customer satisfaction through early and continuous delivery of valuable software; delivering working software frequently, from every couple of weeks to every couple of months; and making the delivery of working software the primary measure of progress. For more information on the Agile framework, see http://www.agilealliance.org.

[c]A sprint is a block of time during which the software development team works to create a potentially usable piece of functionality. GCSS-J's sprints lasted 20 days.

[d]A Milestone Decision Authority is an acquisition official with the authority to approve a program's entry into the next phase of the acquisition process.

Table 5: Manufacturing Operations Management Project (MOMentum)—Critical Success Factors

Critical success factor	Description
Project manager experience with business processes This supports the commonly identified critical success factor: *Program staff had the necessary knowledge and skills.*	National Nuclear Security Administration (NNSA) officials stated that the use of a project manager from the end user organization with decades of experience on the shop floor and an awareness of how the work on the shop floor is done was critical to the success of the program. According to the officials, this gave them the ability to ensure that the requirements were fully understood prior to the implementation of the technology.
Project team empowerment	NNSA officials stated that the project team was empowered to take prudent risks, suggest new and improved approaches to meeting the required deliverables, and minimize activities that did not add value. For example, the team members were allowed to continue doing work while requirements were pending approval by the oversight board.
Developer flexibility	NNSA officials noted that the project's discrete work efforts—and associated cost, schedule, and scope commitments—were defined and managed at the highest possible level. This flexibility provided the developers with the ability to use whatever solutions and practices they thought were best to meet the needs of the end user.
Project team and contractor communication This supports the commonly identified critical success factor: *Program officials maintained regular communications with the prime contractor.*	According to NNSA officials, the potential risks of the developer's enhanced flexibility were balanced by increased communication with the project team. Specifically, the project managers from the government and developer met every week; the integrated project team[a]—which consisted of both government and developer staff—met multiple times each week; and the full MOMentum team, including government and developer staff, as well as other stakeholders, met quarterly.
Commercial off-the-shelf software compatibility	NNSA officials stated that the decision to purchase the commercial off-the-shelf software package that was most compatible with their existing system was a critical success factor. Although other commercial off-the-shelf packages might have provided superior functionality, NNSA officials determined that it would have been more difficult to integrate those other packages with their existing system.
Early acquisition of commercial off-the-shelf software	NNSA officials stated that the early acquisition of the commercial off-the-shelf software contributed to their success in two ways. First, because they were able to purchase the software during a time that the vendor was offering lower than normal prices, they were able to save millions of dollars on the purchase price and related licensing fees. Second, had they not acquired the software early, they would have developed their solution using a different software product, and then would have migrated that solution onto the intended software product once it was purchased. The early acquisition enabled NNSA to avoid having to migrate the solution from one product to another, thus saving time and money.
Prioritized requirements This supports the commonly identified critical success factor: *Program staff prioritized requirements.*	The program's requirements were divided into three tiers based on mission need. This allowed the program officials to prioritize the requirements and adjust the scope of the program based on the capabilities of the software. According to NNSA officials, the first tier contained mission-essential requirements, the second tier contained requirements that would only be completed if funds were available after tier one requirements were satisfied, and the third tier contained requirements that were not mission critical and would only be met if the commercial off-the-shelf software addressed them without any custom coding.

Critical success factor	Description
Knowledge and experience of project team This supports the commonly identified critical success factor: *Program staff had the necessary knowledge and skills.*	According to an NNSA official, the SAP[b] team at Y-12 is cited for their superior performance in SAP literature due to the complexity of the implementation and its low operating costs. Additionally, the core SAP development team at Y-12 has been working together for over a decade as the result of limited turnover.
Proactive communications with stakeholders This supports the commonly identified critical success factor: *Program officials were actively engaged with stakeholders.*	According to an NNSA official, proactive communications with stakeholders led to increased transparency. This transparency led to alternative and tailored approaches being reviewed and approved by stakeholders prior to their implementation. Additionally, the transparency contributed to a collegial, non-toxic work environment.
Tailored independent reviews based on project risk	According to an NNSA official, instead of having a large, comprehensive review of the entire program, they brought in a number of expert consultants to conduct smaller, targeted reviews of the portions of the program that had the highest risks. For example, an expert in the commercial software product used for the project helped the program to validate the team's approach for modifying the software. Consequently, the program was able to limit changes to the software; this decreases the risk of a commercial product being modified to the point that it becomes a one-of-a-kind, customized solution that is no longer supported by new releases of the vendor's product, thus becoming costly to maintain.
Business owner participation in requirements development This supports the commonly identified critical success factor: *End users and stakeholders were involved in the development of requirements.*	According to an NNSA official, including the business owners in requirements development ensured that the system requirements addressed the end users' needs and that program funding would be spent on things that would contribute to meeting those needs. NNSA officials stated that obtaining feedback from the end user was facilitated by having end user representatives serve on the investment review board.
Early end user validation of functionality This supports the commonly identified critical success factor: *Users participated in testing of system functionality prior to formal user acceptance.*	MOMentum officials stated that the end users' early testing of the system's interfaces and functionality was critical to the success of the investment. Specifically, the program used conference room pilots to allow stakeholders to validate that the developers had captured all of the requirements and that the implementation of the requirements in the software was adequate. This allowed feedback to be received early in the design process where mistakes or misinterpretations could be corrected more economically than if they were discovered later during formal system testing.

Source: GAO analysis of agency data.

[a]The Office of Management and Budget defines an integrated project team as a multi-disciplinary team led by a project manager responsible and accountable for planning, budgeting, procurement and life-cycle management of the investment to achieve its cost, schedule, and performance goals. Team skills include budgetary, financial, capital planning, procurement, user, program, architecture, earned value management, security, and other staff as appropriate.

[b]SAP is a company that develops commercial software under the same name. This software consists of multiple, integrated functional modules that perform a variety of business-related tasks.

Table 6: Western Hemisphere Travel Initiative (WHTI)—Critical Success Factors

Critical success factor	Description
Leadership exhibited urgency and commitment This supports the commonly identified critical success factor: *Senior department and agency executives supported the programs.*	According to U.S. Customs and Border Protection (CBP) officials, senior leadership committed to implementing WHTI at land and sea ports of entry by June 1, 2009. The WHTI program manager stated that this deadline resulted in greater involvement of senior Department of Homeland Security (DHS) and CBP leadership. For example, the program manager told us that a former Deputy Secretary reached out to another agency when that agency's efforts to collaborate on an issue were not meeting the schedule requirements of the WHTI program. That official told us that after receiving the necessary support from the other department, CBP was able to more rapidly query that department's data.
Congressional support through funding This supports the commonly identified critical success factor: *Programs received sufficient funding.*	The WHTI program manager stated that the WHTI program received the requested funding from Congress for the 2 years leading up to the June 1, 2009, implementation date. Additionally, that official told us that Congress provided 2-year money, that is, money that could be obligated over a period of 2 years. Officials told us that the 2-year money gave the program great flexibility to accommodate the inherent complexities and expenditures incurred in a multiyear deployment, and to adapt to inevitable modifications in deployment requirements (that is, additional sites, lanes, and functionality).
Program office control of WHTI budget	CBP officials explained that the WHTI program budget was controlled by the WHTI program manager. Those officials stated that the WHTI program manager agreed on spending limits with the CBP offices that supported WHTI (e.g., facilities and technology) and monitored the expenditures. In contrast, CBP officials explained that funds are traditionally allocated to the CBP offices that support programs by the CBP Office of Administration. This arrangement reduces business sponsor oversight and control.
Program manager leadership	CBP officials explained that the WHTI program office was led by an experienced program manager. Those officials explained that the WHTI program manager created the necessary environment for the team to succeed. One official added that the WHTI program manager's leadership inspired the WHTI team.
Program office knowledge This supports the commonly identified critical success factor: *Program staff had the necessary knowledge and skills.*	CBP officials explained that the WHTI program was supported by experienced staff members. CBP officials stated that almost every member of the WHTI team had a good understanding of acquisitions (demonstrated by some staff holding acquisition certifications) and program management. Further, those officials told us that the team always had two members who were knowledgeable on a particular issue—one team member was responsible for the issue and the other was a backup in the event that the primary member was not available. These skills contributed to effective program oversight of the WHTI contractors through all phases of the acquisition, not just during contract award. Moreover, one official attributed the unity of the team and the commitment to work collaboratively to the respect that each team member had for others.
Program office staff familiarity and stability This supports the commonly identified critical success factor: *Government and contractor staff were consistent and stable.*	CBP officials stated that many team members worked together on previous projects. As a result, those officials said that these team members already knew each other's role, skills, and work style, and this familiarity enabled the program office to quickly perform at a high level. Those officials added that key staff members—such as the WHTI technical leader—remained consistent throughout the WHTI program. The low turnover of WHTI program staff helped to maintain that high performance. Moreover, according to a CBP official, the staff genuinely liked to work with one another and were able to collaborate effectively.

Critical success factor	Description
Stakeholder involvement This supports the commonly identified critical success factor: *Program officials were actively engaged with stakeholders.*	CBP officials told us that the WHTI integrated project team was formed before the completion of planning efforts and well before the initiation of development efforts. According to CBP officials, the WHTI integrated project team was composed of numerous stakeholders such as legal support and representatives from budget/finance. CBP officials added that the team was formed prior to acquisition and development efforts, and weekly and later biweekly meetings were held with high participation rates. Those officials stated that the integrated project team was a decision-making body—not just a mechanism for the WHTI program office to communicate with stakeholders.
Consistent message when communicating about the program	CBP officials told us that everyone in DHS and CBP—including the DHS Secretary and CBP Commissioner—adhered to WHTI's consistent message and terminology when communicating with Congress, the media, and the American public. This consistent message was used to describe, for example, the goals of the program, deployment plans, privacy implications of the Radio Frequency Identification (RFID) infrastructure, and impact of the program on select groups crossing the border, including U.S. and Canadian children and Native Americans.
Daily coordination with the prime contractor during deployment This supports the commonly identified critical success factor: *Program officials maintained regular communication with the prime contractor.*	CBP officials explained that key WHTI officials participated in a 9:00 a.m. daily teleconference with the contractor while WHTI was being deployed to ensure proper coordination and the rapid resolution of problems. CBP officials explained that this daily coordination was necessary given that deployment had a significant impact on port-of-entry operations; namely, each lane was taken offline for 1 to 2 days while the infrastructure was deployed. For example, an official told us that the electric system which provided power to the lanes at a port of entry was not adequate. This official said that the issue was identified and raised during the daily morning conference, someone was assigned to begin working on the problem during that meeting, and the issue was resolved.
Prioritization of planning	CBP officials explained that their initial instinct given the aggressive implementation timeline was to focus on technical solutions, developmental efforts, and deployment. However, those officials stated that the WHTI program began with, and completed, key planning efforts which eventually secured the success of the program. Examples of these planning efforts include policy changes, regulatory requirements, and process reengineering changes.
Well-planned acquisition approach; active contract management	CBP officials explained that the program obtained extensive input from potential contractors on WHTI requirements as a result of those potential contractors' review of the draft statement of work for the WHTI design, procurement, testing, and deployment of the RFID/ License Plate Reader (LPR) infrastructure. Those officials stated that questions from the potential contractors improved the quality of the request for proposals and the resulting contract. Additionally, CBP officials explained that they utilized a fixed-price structure for the above-mentioned contract. Those officials said that this structure reduced the government's risk of realizing cost overruns. Further, CBP officials stated that the contracting officer for that contract was colocated with program office officials. As a result, CBP officials explained that the contracting officer was fully aware of operational issues and requirements, provided needed guidance, and expedited contract modifications.

Critical success factor	Description
Testing prior to deployment This supports the commonly identified critical success factor: *Users participated in testing of system functionality prior to formal user acceptance.*	CBP officials explained that the program's testing prior to deployment was critical to the success of the WHTI program. In particular, those officials stated that the LPR and RFID design and performance were tested at a mock port-of-entry test facility constructed at an old private airport in Virginia. CBP officials said that these test lanes with RFID and LPR infrastructure were used to optimize the system so that it (1) would be able to detect multiple RFID cards in one vehicle within that lane, and (2) would not be overly sensitive as to detect RFID cards from other lanes. Additionally, those officials explained that numerous vehicle speeds, models (e.g., sedans, sports cars, SUVs, etc.), and license plate types were used to test the LPR and associated camera technologies. Further, according to CBP officials, tests were done in all weather and lighting conditions to ensure the cameras could capture acceptable images under all circumstances. Moreover, those officials told us that a group of core end users was brought to this facility to test the forthcoming technology. As a result, CBP officials explained that when many of these end users returned to their ports of entry, they became advocates for the WHTI technology.
Funding for public outreach	CBP officials stated that they believe that Congress's recognition of the significant social and cultural changes required of U.S. and Canadian citizens to successfully implement WHTI led Congress to appropriate funding for an effective communications and outreach campaign to increase awareness about new requirements for travel documents. CBP officials stated that this campaign, which relied on professional advertising media (e.g., TV, print, radio, and billboard advertising) provided by a private public relations firm, was something that normally would not be funded for a federal program, but was critical in obtaining buy-in from the local border communities and the traveling public, thus ensuring the success of the program. CBP officials explained that WHTI deployed millions of dollars in technology; however, if travelers did not obtain RFID-enabled travel documents, the technology would be underutilized. According to the WHTI program manager, because of these outreach efforts, WHTI had a compliance rate of 90 percent on the first day that WHTI documents were required to be presented at the land border.
Just-in-time operational and technical training	CBP officials told us that the end users were trained just prior to, during, and immediately after, deployment. Those officials noted that even after the lanes were accepted by CBP officials at the ports of entry, WHTI program officials stayed with the end users for 5 to 7 days to ensure that the end users were fully prepared to use the system. Those officials told us that by the time WHTI was fully implemented, over 10,000 officers had been trained in new operating procedures, application use, and familiarization with the new lane equipment and travel documents.

Source: GAO analysis of agency data.

Table 7: Integrated Terminal Weather System (ITWS)—Critical Success Factors

Critical success factor	Description
Program manager leadership	Federal Aviation Administration (FAA) officials told us that having ITWS program manager leadership that was organized, firm, and had integrity contributed to making ITWS successful. For example, those officials told us that the former program manager vigorously defended the program's budget when presenting it to senior management.
Support of senior leadership This supports the commonly identified critical success factor: *Senior department and agency executives supported the program.*	FAA officials explained that the FAA Joint Resources Council and Executive Council provided good support for the program. For example, individuals on these councils provided advice and guidance regarding acquisition procedures as well as fostering the development of leadership skills.
Consistency of program manager This supports the commonly identified critical success factor: *Government and contractor staff were consistent and stable.*	The program retained the same program manager for 7 years to oversee the development and deployment of the system, which provided continuity.
Development and prioritization of requirements This supports the following two commonly identified critical success factors: *End users and stakeholders were involved in the development of requirements* and *Program staff prioritized requirements.*	FAA officials told us that ITWS end users in Orlando presented the development team with a "wish list" of requirements that would help them significantly. For example, the end users identified the need for forecasts at 10-, 20-, and 60-minute intervals. In addition, the requirements were prioritized by a team of end users and developers based on balancing their importance to the end users and the maturity of the technology.
Testing of prototypes This supports the commonly identified critical success factor: *Users participated in testing of system functionality prior to formal user acceptance.*	FAA officials stated that conceptual displays for future ITWS capabilities were presented to end users in the field. Those officials explained that these efforts helped to ensure that the end users' needs would be addressed by the operational ITWS solution.
Regular stakeholder involvement This supports the commonly identified critical success factor: *Program officials were actively engaged with stakeholders.*	The ITWS program involved stakeholders (e.g., air traffic controller labor representatives, field users, National Weather Service, Department of Defense) by inviting them to meetings every other week. Through these meetings, the former program manager explained that the program was able to obtain the stakeholder buy-in to the ITWS program.
Alignment of knowledge/expertise with tasks This supports the commonly identified critical success factor: *Program staff had the necessary knowledge and skills.*	The former ITWS program manager explained that tasks were assigned to individuals who possessed the requisite knowledge and skills. Additionally, the former program manager stated that he took steps to ensure that his staff could dedicate all of their time to the ITWS program. For example, that official told us that he utilized support contractors that were dedicated to the ITWS program.
Expectations and rewards for success	The former ITWS program manager stated that he provided the ITWS teams with a clear vision, objectives, and expectations during meetings. Additionally, that official told us that he instituted reward programs to provide incentives for the staff to be creative and get things done quickly.
Communication between the program management office team and the program manager	The former ITWS program manager told us that he encouraged the team to share all information with him—both successes and problems. That official told us that this environment made him aware of problems early; as a result, he was able to mitigate the impact of those problems before it became severe.
Continuous schedule management	The former ITWS program manager explained that he relied heavily on the program schedule in order to manage the program. That official added that he ensured that the official responsible for maintaining the program's schedule was present during all of the team's meetings.

Critical success factor	Description
Understanding of personality types This supports the commonly identified critical success factor: *Program staff had the necessary knowledge and skills.*	The former program manager for ITWS stated that the Myers-Briggs Type Indicator contributed to his ability to successfully lead the program. Specifically, that official told us that his training in the Myers-Briggs Type Indicator area helped him to understand how to communicate effectively with individuals of different types, which individuals were the best fit for a particular assignment, and who was the right person to contact to get things done on time.

Source: GAO analysis of agency data.

Table 8: Customer Account Data Engine 2 (CADE 2)—Critical Success Factors

Critical success factor	Description
Senior leadership support This supports the following two commonly identified critical success factors: *Senior department and agency executives supported the programs* and *Programs received sufficient funding.*	Internal Revenue Service (IRS) officials explained that endorsement for CADE 2 has come from the highest levels of the organization. In particular, the IRS Commissioner has made the program one of his top priorities. Those officials told us that the Commissioner, through, for example, his keynote speech at a CADE 2 town hall meeting for IRS employees, has provided a clear and unwavering message about CADE 2, which has unified IRS employees, driven change, and removed barriers that can often impede programs of this magnitude. Additionally, those officials told us that the Commissioner has helped the program obtain funding for CADE 2 by speaking with Congress to sustain interest and support for the program. In addition to support from the Commissioner, IRS officials stated that they have received guidance and support from the IRS Chief Technology Officer since the program's inception. For example, those officials said that CADE 2 leadership meets with the Chief Technology Officer on a monthly basis to discuss the program.
Right mix of people This supports the commonly identified critical success factor: *Program staff had the necessary knowledge and skills.*	IRS officials stated that CADE 2 leadership contains an appropriate mix of government executives that have been recruited from within and outside of IRS. Those officials explained that individuals recruited from inside IRS provide institutional knowledge and expertise on current legacy and past modernization efforts, enterprise architecture, enterprise IT operations currently in place, tax administration processes, and general administrative procedures such as hiring and budget formulation. With regard to CADE 2 executives that were recruited from external sources, IRS officials stated that the Treasury Secretary utilized his authority to authorize critical pay positions[a] for CADE 2. Officials stated that those executives have come into the IRS with demonstrated success in managing large-scale transformation efforts in accordance with best practices. For example, those officials told us that the CADE 2 program manager was previously responsible for the design, development, and implementation of several major global information technology solutions for a major corporation.
Right-sized governance model	IRS officials told us that in comparison to other IRS business system modernization projects, the governance model for CADE 2 has been streamlined. For example, those officials stated that the CADE 2 governance structure includes an executive steering committee (ESC). This committee consists of senior executives from Modernization and Information Technology Services, business partners, and the Department of the Treasury, and serves as an oversight group that ensures the program stays aligned with the IRS strategic plan and approves decisions with significant organizational or external impact. IRS officials explained that, in contrast to other programs at IRS that utilize an ESC, the CADE 2 ESC is dedicated solely to the CADE 2 program. Those officials told us that this gives an added measure of accountability and responsibility for the successful outcome of the program. Additionally, IRS officials explained that because the ESC is dedicated solely to CADE 2, there is only one layer of governance below it—the Governance Board. This board consists of Associate Chief Information Officers from CADE 2 Applications Development, Enterprise Operations, Enterprise Services, and the business modernization executive from the business partner. The board ensures that objectives are met, decisions and issues are resolved in a timely manner, risks are managed appropriately, and the expenditure of resources allocated is fiscally sound. According to IRS officials, having only one layer of governance below the ESC enhances accountability and streamlines decision making and management of risks and issues. In addition to the two previously mentioned bodies, the CADE 2 program utilizes advisory councils for guidance and assistance in key areas.

Critical success factor	Description
Program office as system integrator	According to IRS officials, CADE 2 is the first program of its size and magnitude where the IRS has acted as the integrator and program manager over the acquisition since its inception. Consequently, those officials told us that there is a great deal of pride within IRS because employees, rather than outside contractors, are in charge of the integration and management of this substantial technology investment. Officials explained that IRS has established clear lines of authority and accountability between the CADE 2 program office (integrator), the business partners, and the delivery partners (i.e., the organizations within IRS Modernization and Information Technology Services directly responsible for the CADE 2 projects). Those officials noted that the program manager brought in a coach to drive the program office, delivery partners, and business partners to improve leadership and communication skills.
Integrated project management processes	IRS officials explained that, as the CADE 2 integrator, they have established a program framework for ensuring integration of the two projects—daily processing and database implementation—at the program level. Specifically, those officials stated that they have developed a program life-cycle framework for the CADE 2 program, which includes clearly defined life-cycle phases, milestones, artifacts, and reviews. IRS officials noted that this framework enables the program office to manage the CADE 2 projects in a coordinated and integrated manner. Additionally, those officials told us that they have enhanced program management processes— such as risk management, scheduling, and requirements management—in order to account for integration at the program level. For example, IRS officials stated that they use a software tool to manage their requirements. Those officials told us that, using this tool, they now trace requirements from design through testing.
Project planning to set solid program foundation	IRS officials explained that they established four key documents in the early stages of the program: (1) a program charter, which defines the mission and goals of the CADE 2 program; (2) a solutions architecture, which describes the existing and target business processes and solutions architecture; (3) a program roadmap, which describes IRS's plan to transition from the current state to the Target State for CADE 2; and (4) a program management plan, which describes the practices and principles used to manage the program. Those officials explained that these four documents kept the team focused, and provided stability and guidance for the program.
Establishment of key milestones and decision points	IRS officials stated that during an early milestone for Transition State 1, the IRS Chief Technology Officer asked the program to clearly define the path that IRS needed to take in order to fully implement the first transition state within the planned time frame. This definition included a framework of activities which includes go/no-go decision points, deep dive reviews, independent readiness reviews, and internal confidence assessments using a confidence scoring methodology to fully inform assessments. IRS officials noted that these activities included reviews by parties external to IRS. Those officials told us that the effort to define the framework drove the program to plan more proactively for deployment at the completion of logical design review. IRS officials stated that this early deployment planning was beneficial because it provided accountability, drove contingency planning, and enhanced risk management.

Critical success factor	Description
Consistent and open communication This supports the commonly identified critical success factor: *Program officials were actively engaged with the stakeholders.*	IRS officials explained that they regularly report the status of CADE 2 internally to IRS employees working on the program, delivery and business partner executives, and stakeholders. For example, those officials told us that feedback forums have been established for employees and stakeholders to submit questions and obtain clarifications on the program. Further, in anticipation of the forthcoming changes associated with the January 2012 deployment of the Transition State 1 solution, IRS established a communications working group to coordinate and collaborate on CADE 2 and related IRS programs. Those officials explained that this open environment has quashed secrets and hidden agendas. Additionally, IRS officials stated that CADE 2 information is frequently shared with entities external to IRS, including oversight bodies, audit entities, and external tax advisory groups. Examples of the types of information provided include: plans, progress made, risk mitigation strategies, and information relating to the program's cost, schedule, and scope.
Use of existing contracts	IRS officials stated that because significant time is required in order to establish a new contract, IRS has utilized existing contracts to support CADE 2. Those contracts are used for activities such as program management support and technical support. Those officials noted that the use of existing contracts allowed the IRS to achieve economies of scale for large purchases. Additionally, IRS officials stated that they have been able to take advantage of the skills and expertise of contractors that have worked on the current program. For example, contract personnel with experience in creating the database that supports the current program are supporting the development of the database that will support CADE 2.

Source: GAO analysis of agency data.

[a]Critical position pay authority allows department leadership to set the rate of basic pay for a given critical position.

Table 9: Occupational Health Record-keeping System (OHRS)—Critical Success Factors

Critical success factor	Description
Project team/end user representative partnership This supports the following two commonly identified critical success factors: *Program officials were actively engaged with stakeholders* and *Program staff had the necessary knowledge and skills.*	Veterans Affairs (VA) officials stated that the project was jointly owned by the end users and the project team. The end user representative was involved in daily team status meetings, various requirements development activities, and lessons-learned reviews. She was involved in decision making for things such as user interface screens and user training. As a result, the end user representative was treated as part of the project team instead of as a customer who would only be involved at the beginning or the very end of the project.
Senior leadership support This supports the commonly identified critical success factor: *Senior department and agency executives supported the programs.*	VA officials noted that senior leadership involvement was critical to the success of the acquisition. In particular, the Chief of the Office of Public Health and Environmental Hazards (located within the Veteran's Health Administration (VHA)) was committed to the success of the program and helped the program get its funding. Additionally, the Chief Consultant of the Occupational Health Strategic Healthcare Group allowed the end user representative to devote a significant amount of her time to OHRS. Furthermore, the VA Chief Information Officer and his staff participated in the early discussions regarding the need to implement OHRS.
Requirements development, prioritization, and analysis This supports the following two commonly identified critical success factors: *End users and stakeholders were involved in the development of requirements* and *Program staff prioritized requirements.*	VA officials stated that the end user representative identified a set of requirements for an occupational health system 3 years prior to the initiation of OHRS development efforts. This was critical to the success of the program because the team did not have to start requirements development from scratch. Prior to the implementation of these requirements, the end user representative and six additional subject matter experts analyzed the requirements to ensure that they were still valid given the length of time since they were initially identified. A VA official also stated that the priorities of the requirements were initially defined, then reviewed and changed throughout the project development life cycle. For example, at times it was discovered that there were requirements that needed to be implemented in conjunction with other requirements due to dependencies that were discovered later during the development.
Early end user testing of functionality This supports the commonly identified critical success factor: *End users participated in testing of system functionality prior to formal user acceptance.*	The end user representative tested functionality on a daily basis, approved features when they were completed at the end of each sprint, and formally approved products prior to their release. The team was able to complete quality assurance testing more quickly because the end user representative tested the product prior to the system going through more formal quality assurance testing.
Continuous risk management	VA officials stated that the risk management strategy that the program used was critical to its success. According to the VA officials, risks were identified at daily team meetings, and mitigation strategies were determined by the program management office when possible. Furthermore an official explained that risk management is built into Agile software development.[a] For example, by involving the end user early and often, VA decreased the risk that the end user would not be satisfied with the final product.
Early involvement of implementation staff	VA officials stated that bringing a member of the VA team who performs final testing and deployment onto the OHRS team early contributed to the success of the program. Specifically, those officials told us that the process of final testing and deployment was completed sooner for OHRS than some other VA systems.

Critical success factor	Description
Constant tracking of progress	VA officials stated that they used standardized software tools to measure and track progress of the work being done, and the associated schedule and cost. For example, the team used a software tool called "VersionOne" to track the daily progress of the development team in addressing program requirements and testing software. In addition, they used another software tool called "TeamPlay" to measure the project's major milestones, costs, and earned value on a weekly and monthly basis. The ability to manage progress contributed to the investment's success.
Project team knowledge This supports the commonly identified critical success factor: *Program staff had the necessary knowledge and skills.*	VA officials indicated that the selection of team members based on their knowledge of VHA programs, skill sets, and desire to be on an Agile team contributed to the success of the program. For example, VA officials explained that the entire team—including the end user representative—was trained in Agile software development. Those officials noted that this training was reinforced by the team's use of an Agile "coach"—an individual that audited the team's Agile processes and who provided suggestions that improved the team's performance. Additionally, VA officials stated that the end user representative trained the OHRS technical staff on issues relating to occupational health and why implementation of OHRS was important.
Relationship with contractor This supports the commonly identified critical success factor: *Program officials maintained regular communication with the prime contractor.*	VA officials stated that the partnership between the government and contractor contributed to the success of the program. An official stated that the contractor and the program management office staff (in addition to the end user) met daily, which ensured they were all kept apprised of the program's status. Moreover, an official stated that the relationship between the program office and the contractor was not adversarial, which was necessary for the blended team of contractor, end user, and VA information technology staff to be successful.
Definition of performance measures	Performance measures were defined in the contract and were used by both the program management office and the contractor
Inclusion of the contractor in planning and scheduling	According to VA officials, including the contractor in the planning and scheduling of deliverables contributed to the success of the program because it helped to ensure that the deliverables were on time.

Source: GAO analysis of agency data.

[a]Agile software development is not a set of tools or a single methodology, but a philosophy based on selected values, such as prioritizing customer satisfaction through early and continuous delivery of valuable software; delivering working software frequently, from every couple of weeks to every couple of months; and making the delivery of working software the primary measure of progress. For more information on the Agile framework, see http://www.agilealliance.org.

Appendix III: GAO Contact and Staff Acknowledgments

GAO Contact	David A. Powner, (202) 512-9286 or pownerd@gao.gov
Staff Acknowledgments	In addition to the contact named above, Deborah A. Davis (Assistant Director), Kaelin P. Kuhn, Lee McCracken, Thomas E. Murphy, Jamelyn Payan, and Andrew Stavisky made key contributions to this report.

www.ingramcontent.com/pod-product-compliance
Lightning Source LLC
Chambersburg PA
CBHW081243180526
45171CB00005B/524